JOHN HERDMAN

Voice Without Restraint

A STUDY OF
BOB DYLAN'S LYRICS AND
THEIR BACKGROUND

PAUL HARRIS PUBLISHING

EDINBURGH

ACKNOWLEDGEMENTS

I am more than grateful for the stimulation provided over the years by conversation with other Dylan enthusiasts, and in particular I wish to thank the following for their invaluable help and suggestions during the writing of this book: Alan Barr, Andrew Greig, Noeleen Grindle and Rory Watson.

First published 1982 in Great Britain by

PAUL HARRIS PUBLISHING
40 York Place
Edinburgh

The publisher acknowledges the financial assistance of the Scottish Arts Council in the publication of this volume.

ISBN 0 86228 019 2 Cased
ISBN 0 86228 037 0 Limp

Photoset printed and bound in Great Britain by
REDWOOD BURN LIMITED
Trowbridge, Wiltshire

CONTENTS

Chapter One

Introductory

In probably the most lucid passage in Bob Dylan's novel *Tarantula* – a work of which lucidity is not the prime characteristic – a "butter sculptor" named Snowplow Floater delivers a funny and extremely cutting dismissal of a critic of his work.[1] It is a passage which any prospective critic of the songs of Dylan would do well to read, and one calculated to make him think twice before starting. "Do you know what it feels like to make some butter sculpture?" Floater demands, "do you know what it feels like to actually ooze that butter around & create something of fantastic worth?" He announces his indifference to the critic's opinions, telling him that he takes himself too seriously and will end up in hospital with an ulcer; " – just remember, tho", he advises him before signing off, "when you evaluate a piece of butter, you are talking about yourself, so you'd just better sign your name..." Elsewhere in the same book Dylan suggests that "nothing is worth analyzing – you learn from a conglomeration of the incredible past".[2]

He is right to be wary. "The point is not understanding what I write but feeling it", he once told an interviewer,[3] and this protestation voices a basic truth: Dylan's art must be "understood" primarily on the nerves. The attempt to substitute a cerebral comprehension for a felt response, which is really what Dylan is condemning, in fact makes real understanding impossible. But true understanding does not negate feeling; on the contrary, it arises entirely from it. The question of the ultimate value of criticism applies, of course, to all art, though it may seem especially pertinent and pressing when we are dealing with an art that is as *immediate* as Dylan's. I have no doubt, though, that it *has* value. As is the case with all artists, there are doubtless some aspects of Dylan's creation which were unconscious and spontaneous in the making, others which were quite deliberate and even calculated; but in no case is the process magical by which feelings and emotions are translated into symbols apprehensible by the senses; this occurs in concrete, specific ways, even though the process may have been instinctive or subliminal for the artist. In criticism, besides, we define the content of art first of all by defining our response to it. It is how the artist

1

impels our response that is of primary interest; and in understanding how we respond we make that response richer and more conscious – which does *not* mean less feeling. Understanding as a substitute for feeling could only be *mis*understanding.

The present study owes a great debt to Michael Gray's *Song and Dance Man – The Art of Bob Dylan,* which is far and away the best and most serious extended examination of Dylan's work that we have. Gray established beyond question that Dylan's creative importance could be demonstrated by critical analysis, and also provided invaluable material on his background in the folk tradition, pop music and the rock revolution. The form of my own book is therefore very much determined by what Michael Gray has and has not already done. In the first place, *Song and Dance Man* takes the story only as far as 1970, and I want to bring it up to date by examining the very important work of the past decade which takes in, I believe, one of the peaks of Dylan's achievement. I shall not disregard the earlier years, about which, as with the work of any great artist, there will always be more to say, but proportionately the study will be weighted more on the side of the later albums. I shall also concentrate much more upon Dylan's own output than upon his background, mainly because of the work already done in this field by Michael Gray and others but partly also because I think there is still too much stress laid on Dylan as a representative figure of his time and too little on the songs which make him pre-eminent and for which, more than for any "public" role, he will in the long run be remembered.

This book, again, is primarily a study of the lyrics rather than the music. In examining Dylan's hybrid art some degree of specialisation is probably inevitable, and for my own part I readily admit that I lack the expertise and the critical vocabulary to discuss the musical aspects adequately. I think, that is, that I understand on my nerves what Dylan is doing musically but I cannot intellectualise my response. What is important when dealing with one particular aspect of an artist's work is not in the process to falsify the other aspects. Dylan is primarily a song writer and not a visual poet and his lyrics cannot be dealt with in the same way that one would deal with poetry intended for the eye. As Michael Gray has put it, "it ought to be kept in mind that the selection and organisation of Dylan's language is governed by the artistic disciplines of a medium not solely linguistic or literary . . . Structurally the words of a song differ necessarily from those of a poem. They are not the sole arbiters of their own intended effects, rhythmically or in less technical ways."[4] In considering the sense of the lyrics (which is something more than their "meaning") I shall therefore always ask myself: what is the *voice* saying, what is the *music* saying? Does my under-

2

standing square with *that*? And, of course, all my impressions come first of all from listening to Dylan, not from reading him.

George Steiner, in the course of an examination of the decline of verbal culture in the West attendant upon the decay of religious belief, has suggested at some length that we have entered a period in which "a sound-culture seems to be driving back the old authority of verbal order."[5] "The literacies of popular and classical music", he shows, "informed by new techniques of reproduction not less important than was the spread of cheap mass-printing in its time, are entering our lives at numerous, shaping levels. In many settings and sensibilities, they are providing a 'culture outside the word'." Steiner indicates, too, that this development may represent a natural turning-back towards elements which form the very foundations of human culture. "Conceivably, an ancient circle is closing. Lévi-Strauss has asserted that melody holds the key to the *'mystère suprème de l'homme'*. Grasp the riddle of melodic invention, of our apparently imprinted sense of harmonic accord, and you will touch on the roots of human consciousness. Only music, says Lévi-Strauss, is a primal universal language, at once comprehensible to all and untranslatable into any other idiom. Speech comes later than music; even before the disorder at Babel, it was part of the Fall of man. This supposition is, itself, immemorial."

It is within this context, the context of Marshall McLuhan's "global village" dominated by electronic communications, that the art-form developed pre-eminently by Dylan takes on its importance. For it is precisely by joining itself once more to music that verbal culture may assure its own continuance. Nietzsche showed in *The Birth of Tragedy* that the emergence of Western literary forms was fundamentally involved with "the spirit of music". It seems clear that there is a connection between the present attenuation and exhaustion of these forms and their almost total divergence from their musical roots. The popularity of poetry readings may stem from a sense of the inappropriateness to contemporary social conditions of a literature based entirely on the private response of individual reader to writer. Yet the limitations and snares of this cult are immense, and arise from the unsuitability of the reading as a medium for the communication of visual poetry whose structure is primarily determined by the conditions of print. The restoration to the ear of a more important role among the senses, which has been effected by the coming of the electronic media and which to some extent counters the long dominance of the eye, has been the occasion for the word to resume its old association with the principle of melody. Dylan's art combines literary and musical elements in an inseparable whole and in conditions of the most intimate interdependence, in a way that has not been familiar in the literate culture

3

of the West since before the invention of printing.

That is not of course to deny that Dylan has had his precursors in the popular music of this century, not to mention the oral traditions of non-literate peoples. The point is that his relation to the traditions of "high" or "élite" art is quite different from – and closer than – those of such precursors. Again, it is true that in his own day he has been only half a step ahead of a host of excellent song-poets and writers of rock lyrics – Jagger and Richards, the Beatles, Joni Mitchell, Robert Hunter, Van Morrison, Randy Newman, Bruce Springsteen and many more. Yet on the one hand it is more than doubtful whether any of these could have done what they have, in the way that they have, without the example of Dylan; and on the other, Dylan remains the best: the most complex and varied, the most widely ranging, the most self-renewing, the deepest. Among all these practitioners of a new and thriving art-form, his stands out as the paradigmatic case. He is the major individual artist who has taken command of the central form of his time, and never can there have been a form which made the work of such an artist available to so huge and so far-flung an audience.

It is not only in the form of his art that Dylan reflects the changing cultural conditions of which Marshall McLuhan was writing in the sixties; he reflects them also in the character of his sensibility. McLuhan is constantly at pains to stress the simultaneity of perception, the consciousness of different levels of experience co-existing, which he believes links "electronic man" with his pre-literate ancestors: "Paradoxically, at this moment in our culture, we meet once more preliterate man. For him there was no subliminal factor in experience; his mythic forms of explanation explicated all levels of any situation at the same time.'"[6] Dylan's songs, in the mosaic structure which they so often exhibit, vividly communicate just such a multi-layered explication, and Dylan has said more than once that such a habit of mind is natural to him. Talking to *Playboy*, for instance, about an abortive documentary called *Eat the Document* made about him in 1966, he observes," . . . the more I looked at the film, the more I realized that you could get more onto film than just one train of thought. My mind works that way, anyway. We tend to work on different levels.'"[7] And replying to a *Rolling Stone* question about the different levels noticeable in his songs, he replies, "That's right, and that's because my mind and my heart work on all those levels. Shit, I don't want to be chained down to the same old level all the time.'"[8] Dylan's sensibility is not mainly linear and sequential, that is, not based on a mode of perception in which the claims of the eye override those of the other senses; its bias is rather spatial.

Dylan's art has strong links too with the conditions under which, in preliterate cultures, oral poetry was composed. Albert B. Lord has written of these conditions: "Our oral poet is composer. Our singer of tales is a composer of tales. Singer, performer, composer and poet are one under different aspects *but at the same time*. Singing, performing, composing are facets of the same act."[9] With some qualifications, this is true of Dylan: certainly the different functions which Lord enumerates come together in him as in the traditional "singer of tales". Although he composes before he performs, he always in some sense recreates, hence re-composes, his songs in performance. Unlike an oral maker he *writes* his songs, but he does so with a re-creative process in mind, and as David Buchan says, "Oral composition is ... an essentially re-creative process."[10] Speaking of the conditions which obtain when literacy is beginning to overtake the old oral tradition, Buchan notes that "it is possible, at a certain point in the tradition, for a person to be both literate and an oral composer. It is only when a person ceases to be re-creative along traditional lines and accepts the literate concept of the fixed text that he or she can no longer be classed as oral."[11] Dylan, placed at a time when an *aural* mode is beginning to make great inroads upon the assumptions of literacy, works in a similar border-land. In performance he is not tied to any fixed text, but the fact of recording does give certain performances the status of permanency which was denied to the oral makers. His lyrics, again, do appear in print, though the text cannot be regarded as fixed in a strict sense, and this method of publication is in any event very secondary to the aural forms of performance and recording. The fluid, provisional nature of Dylan's songs makes them, in their literary aspect, a notable and important departure from literate tradition. They can be, and are, altered and renewed again and again to conform with new moods, new times, new preoccupations. This quality is entirely dependent on their being cast in an aural rather than a visual mode (unlike contemporary classical music, which remains tied to an established textual form).

Another point which follows from the particular cultural conditions under which Dylan is operating is that his work cannot be abstracted from the way in which *he* interprets it in performance: the "interpretation" is part of the creative essence. Words and music are alike inseparable from their relation to Dylan's voice; performed by others, his songs can sometimes virtually disappear, or at the least become something different and less. They can be said to exist fully only in performance or recording by Dylan. Not only do words which may seem to have a kind of half-life on the page come into their full being when he sings them, but the music is devitalised if we fail to listen to the words it is carrying – and this is something which differentiates Dylan from the majority of rock artists. Ellen

Willis makes the point well when she indicates that, "Words or rhymes that seem gratuitous in print often make good musical sense and Dylan's voice, an extraordinary interpreter of emotion ... makes vague lines clear."[12] What Dylan "means" in a song, also, is not always what the words say: the sense may be conveyed through *tensions* between words, expression and musical mood. Dylan's voice does not just interpret his lyrics, it gives them life. His marvellous timing and breath-control, his capacity for drawing out lines almost to breaking-point, his emotional subtlety and inspired phrasing, make it one of his greatest artistic assets. Its interpenetration with his literary talents must always be kept in mind when thinking about the lyrics.

What is most undeniable about Dylan's achievement over the years is his astonishing – seemingly almost limitless – emotional range, and his power of creative renewal, what Jon Landau has called his "unrelenting capacity to grow".[13] This central creative endowment is intimately related to his unregenerate individualism and his courage in following his own path in the face of extraordinary pressures. There can be few if any artists who have had to reckon with *commercial* pressures of the enormity of those which have been Dylan's lot, in his unique position as a serious major artist who is also – or has been – a popular cultural hero in a global context. His coolness and nerve in coping with them have testified to a formidable integrity. His achievement, too, stands in contradiction to the views of those who see art moving in the direction of collaborative or communal activity: although he works with other musicians, and seems to have a knack of bringing the best out of them, his own personal vision always remains in control. In this sense he looks both ways: his pioneering development of an artform which corresponds to the realities of communication in the modern world is matched by an individualism which links him with traditional concepts of artistic freedom. Ellen Willis has here again been the most far-sighted of his critics: "Dylan is no apostle of the electronic age. Rather, he is a fifth-columnist from the past, shaped by personal and political non-conformity, by blues and modern poetry. He has imposed his commitment to individual freedom (and its obverse, isolation) on the hip passivity of pop culture, his literacy on an illiterate music. He has used the publicity machine to demonstrate his belief in privacy. His songs and public role are guides to survival in the world of the image, the cool and the high. And in coming to terms with that world, he has forced it to come to terms with him."[14]

Much of the discontent and even rage at Dylan's successive artistic revolutions and the accompanying modifications of his image can be traced to a sense of frustration on the part of the media and his fans that he would and will not allow them to own or control him. The chorus of condemnation in the wake of the 1965 Newport Festival in particular, when Dylan demonstrated his move to electric rock, was almost universal, only a few brave voices like that of Paul Nelson asserting that in their preference for Pete Seeger over Dylan the Newport audience had chosen "the safety of wishful thinking rather than the painful, always difficult stab of art."[15] In one of a series of particularly nasty and short-sighted articles Ewan MacColl described Dylan as "a youth of mediocre talent" and his work as "tenth-rate drivel", and with quite singular ineptitude characterised him as representing a "movement" of American song writing "where journalism is more important than art, where flabby sentimentality and shrill self-pity take the place of passion."[16] In this context it is good for a Scotsman to be able to record that a voice in Scotland was raised thus early in defence of Dylan. Hamish Henderson, one of the fathers of the Scottish folk revival, pled that we should be grateful for "the creators, the makers, the composers, those with a spark of the divine fire – if anyone can leaven this unholy lump, they will. And before we start reaching for stones to chuck at Bob Dylan, as if he were a sort of folk-song equivalent of the woman taken in adultery . . . let us for heaven's sake remember that an unmistakable vein of genuine poetry runs through the best of his work . . . The folk scene has been bedevilled not only by the cynical money-grubber – and the witless bonehead – of the commercial revival, but also by the phoney purist: the bloke who poses as the clearer out of an Augean stable into which he himself has tipped a goodly amount of muck."[17]

Henderson's comments have a pertinence which extends beyond the immediate circumstances of that mid-nineteen-sixties quarrel, for it is not only the folk purists who have turned against Dylan when he has moved in a direction they have not approved of: the rock fraternity has proved equally sensitive to his subsequent re-orientations. His "country period" of around 1969–70, when he produced *Nashville Skyline*, *Self Portrait* and *New Morning*, saw his rock following reacting with horror at his adoption of what they saw as a musical style representing the values of "redneck" America, values regarded as diametrically opposed to those he was deemed to have stood for and represented in the nineteen-sixties. It was assumed that Dylan was lost, that he had sold his soul, and could now be discounted as a serious force in popular music. Actually he was reflecting, just as he did in his early "protest" days and again when he voiced the feelings of the streets in his rock heyday, the mood and tendency of American life as it was shortly to reveal itself; and before too long he was to resurface with some of the greatest albums of his career.

7

VOICE WITHOUT RESTRAINT

Now once more, with his conversion to Christianity in 1979 and the issue of *Slow Train Coming*, Dylan is being accused of "betrayal" by his followers, and savaged by the musical press. To cite but one of many possible examples, Michael Goldberg proclaims that "Bob Dylan has left the side of free-thinking, socially aware, sometimes cynical human beings trying to make ethical choices in a modern world ripped apart by the war and prejudice. For him, all is solved in one simple act: accepting God. Where are the de-programmers when we really need them?"[18] As always, there have been honourable exceptions to the predominant trend of reaction, for example Jann Wenner's highly appreciative review of *Slow Train Coming* in *Rolling Stone*,[19] in which he hails the record as one of Dylan's greatest ever. But in general the tone of the response leaves us with a strong and rather depressing sense of *déjà vu*.

All this is not of course to suggest that the country style albums are among Dylan's most notable achievements, or that there are no disturbing tendencies of thought and feeling in *Slow Train Coming*. The point is rather that a tone which we can recognise appears in all these periodic condemnations of Dylan's changes of direction, a tone which goes beyond specific criticism of elements of content. It is a tone of moral outrage, and also distinctly proprietorial. It seems to suggest that Dylan should not be allowed to change and grow (and growth is, need it be said, impossible without change), that if for instance he adopts an "unacceptable" set of beliefs he is betraying those who depend on him for moral leadership, that he should be accountable to his audience for his actions and his attitudes. It is the same old "spokesman for a generation" syndrome which Dylan was obliged to deflate back in 1964–5, and it seems altogether likely that, in addition to the dictates of his own inner needs, one of the factors which precipitates his sometimes startling switches of viewpoint is precisely the need to resist such expectations.

The sense that this argument has been rehearsed before, though in different terms, and that it has always proved to be his detractors who have had to come to terms with Dylan and not vice versa, seems not to impress itself on musical journalists. Dylan himself has said of his Newport experience that "It's like going out to the desert and screaming and then having little kids throw their sandbox at you."[20] It was not – and this is at the heart of the matter – just the *artistic* change which disturbed the little kids; it was the move away from explicit political commentary, from what Dylan himself never called "protest", and especially the abjurance of any public role as spokesman for his generation and of any kind of responsibility other than that of the artist towards his material. His rejection of the simplistic and the superficial in all such contexts, in particular his resistance to all those debilitating tendencies in the modern world which can be associated with the term "journalism", has been radical and undeviating, and his alertness and style in dealing with the entrapments of the media compel our admiration and applause. Ewan MacColl could scarcely have picked a less appropriate way to detract from Dylan's achievement than to suggest that for him "journalism is more important than art", for his nineteen-sixties' interviews are classic documents in the defusing and neutralisation of the journalist, and the art of approaching real issues through exposing the hollowness of stock attitudes. I shall have occasion later to examine in more detail Dylan's relations with the media and with his public.

However little responsibility Dylan has been prepared to accept for his "generation", there can be little doubt that he has modified its consciousness; and not only his own immediate generation but those which have followed it. Again and again he has shown himself uniquely responsive to the underlying pressures and tendencies of his time, to such an extent that he has been able to tell people what they felt before they themselves realised that they were feeling it – which is one reason why so often his public has taken time to catch up with his moves. This kind of sensitivity has amounted on occasions to something like clairvoyance. His most famous anticipation of an actual event relates to the Watergate scandal. In 1974, the year of Nixon's disgrace, Dylan was touring the United States for the first time since his motor cycle accident of 1966. On the *Before the Flood* double concert album recorded live during that tour, he sings "It's Alright, Ma (I'm Only Bleeding)" which contains the lines:

> Goodness hides behind its gates
> But even the president of the United States
> Sometimes must have
> To stand naked.

The words are acknowledged by an overwhelming burst of applause from the audience. The song must have been written nearly ten years earlier, for it was included in *Bringing It All Back Home* which was released in March 1965.

Dylan's central significance is that he has destroyed the notorious gap between "high" and "popular" art. Because he is a rock musician it is natural that his musical background should have received more attention than his literary interests, but one of the keys to his success is that he has combined the instincts of a popular musician, and those which as a song writer he inherits ultimately from the oral composers of songs and ballads, with the very different kinds of approach and activity which belong to the literary writer. He is himself fully aware of this in spite of sometimes claiming the contrary. He has been at pains to play down his "poet" role in many interviews, preferring to refer to himself as a "song and dance man", a "trapeze artist", and even just a "guitar player" – not surprisingly, in view of the approach of most of his questioners. The authors of *Bob Dylan: An Illustrated Discography* have however turned up an October 1965 interview on Radio Detroit in which they quote him as saying (their paraphrase) that "his work can't be called songs any more and that they need a new description as he regards them as a new form of expression".[21]

Dylan has said a number of things on the subject of "influences" which it is as well to bear in mind when touching on the subject of his literary roots. In the poem 'My Life in a Stolen Moment' he observes that "there's too many to mention and I might leave one out"; he acknowledges Woody Guthrie and Big Joe Williams but reminds us that the decisive influences come from the fleeting, multifarious sights and sounds encountered in everyday living:

> Open up yer eyes an' ears an' yer influenced
> an' there's nothing you can do about it . . .

In one of his '11 Outlined Epitaphs' he estimates those influences as "hundreds thousands / perhaps millions". All the same it seems that there were a number of individual artists who made a particularly strong impression at the time his work was becoming fused into that special amalgam of music and poetry peculiar to him. Woody Guthrie's contribution is both well-known and inescapable: his presence behind the early songs is overwhelming, even those in which Dylan's individuality is most assured. Turning to more "literary" figures, Michael Gray adduces by close textual study verbal parallels between Dylan and Blake, Browning and Eliot which are certainly remarkable but which could sometimes reflect coincidence as much as indebtedness. Strangely, though, he makes no mention at all of two European poets whose influence on Dylan is both acknowledged and a matter of copious record, namely Rimbaud and the early Brecht.

It is true that the way these writers affected Dylan is not easily brought out by textual analysis. Apart from one or two rather crude examples their influence is general and diffuse rather than verbally specific. (One such exception is 'The Lonesome Death of Hattie Carroll', which clearly has as a model Brecht's 'Concerning the Infanticide Marie Farrar': not only are there obvious similarities of form and content, but Dylan claims to have made his song in the same way that Brecht made his poem, refashioning the words of a newspaper report.[22]) The influence is none the less important. The poems and ballads in Brecht's first book of verse *Hauspostille* (he used to chant some of them in a harsh and crude voice to his own guitar accompaniment) are a major formative presence behind Dylan's first albums; as Woody Guthrie taught him that a simple song could be a poem, so Brecht taught him that a poem could also be a song. I am sure, again, that the drug-orientated and visionary songs from *Bringing It All Back Home* through *Highway 61 Revisited* to *Blonde on Blonde* are profoundly, if diffusely, influenced by the Rimbaud of *Les Illuminations*.

Perhaps equally important is the effect which the life-styles of these poets had on the formation of Dylan's image (and because of his public situation his projection of successive "images" has a far more intimate relation to Dylan's art than can be imagined for any solely literary figure). The stereotype of the anarchic, antisocial, vagabond poet, which Brecht developed in such early plays as *Baal* and *Im Dickicht der Städte*, was taken directly from Rimbaud (as Martin Esslin points out in his study of Brecht[23]), and Dylan inherited it from both of them. It seems entirely likely too that the mythical adolescence which Dylan invented for himself – repeated flights from home to the freedom of the road – owed something to the realities of Rimbaud's life as well as much to the Woody Guthrie hobo tradition. References to the significance of Rimbaud and Brecht to Dylan's early development can be checked in Anthony Scaduto's biography, but Rimbaud in particular seems to have remained of interest to Dylan throughout the seventies. He is referred to in a song on *Blood on the Tracks*, appears in Dylan's jacket notes for *Desire*, and is mentioned in a 1978 *Playboy* interview.[24] However, all this should not be made too much of: when all is said and done it is the stuff of life which influences an artist most. Having drawn attention to these two writers whose relevance to the formative stages of Dylan's development has been rather overlooked, I shall leave the question of influences aside until the specifics of looking at particular songs dictate otherwise.

In general my concern with Dylan's lyrics will be with how they work rather than with what they mean. Michael Gray is right to assert that "What Dylan does not do ... is to offer a sustained, cohesive philosophy of life, intellectually considered and checked for contradictions."[25] He is too immediate for that, too alive in the moment, and too mercurial. There is however one persistent area of preoccupation with which he is recurrently concerned, and that is religion. It is not (at least until *Slow Train Coming*) something which he sets out to define and elucidate, not a "message" that he strives to convey; rather it is something which will not leave him alone, which again and again obtrudes on his consciousness and asserts its claims through his songs. It represents, in the last resort, a part of his personality which has not been under his control, which repeatedly breaks through into consciousness in the form of persistent themes and obsessive images. As such it is important and interesting enough, or so it appears to me, to be isolated and considered as an autonomous entity in Dylan's art, and a chapter of this book will be devoted to examining it.

Beyond that, I shall make few forays into the risky territory of "interpretation". Dylan has long had to bear the cross of having his songs scoured and dissected in the search for keys and codes, and to some extent he has brought it on himself: the obscurity of much of his writing, together with his undoubted *penchant* for double and hidden meanings, has made this inevitable, and it is beyond question that the songs of the 1965–66 period in particular are full of drug references. The danger however is that when it has been established that drugs (or whatever) are referred to in a certain song, it will be assumed that drugs are what the song is "about". Michael Gray keeps the matter in perspective in the chapter of *Song and Dance Man* called "Theories – Anyone Can Play", but perhaps even his balanced and sceptical treatment is an encouragement of a habit which should be discouraged. For the effect of paying too much heed to the interpretative mania is to inflict damage upon the universality of Dylan's art, to reduce its elasticity of meaning and its open-ended capacity for resonance. Immersion in Dylan's songs has left me convinced that time and again he seeks to leave his meaning open, structures his songs so as to allow each listener to respond according to what is spoken to his or her individual personality.

A couple of examples in one favourite area of speculation – that of sexual aberration – may serve to illustrate how the search for a meaning that is not apparent may rigidify into cryptograms what are in fact songs about recognisable human feelings, for which it is unnecessary and undesirable to supply a restrictive context. Both Craig McGregor and Michael Gray suggest that 'Just Like a Woman' may be about a man,[26] and it is not impossible; but Dylan's delivery of its chorus line "But she breaks just like a little girl" in the *Before the Flood* version certainly belies the position which both these writers take up, that *only* such an interpretation can rescue that line from banality or sentimentality. More ludicrously, McGregor thinks that 'Queen Jane Approximately' may be addressed to a man too (possibly Dylan himself) in spite of the many very strong reasons for assuming the opposite. In support of his argument McGregor adduces the fact that Dylan once told an interviewer that Queen Jane was a man, which he did; but it is as well to take a look, with some sense of Dylan's way with interviewers, at the context. He has been talking seriously and at some length about his electronic music, and in the course of this begins to remark illustratively, "I have this song, 'Queen Jane Approximately' – ". At this point the interviewer impudently cuts in, "Who is Queen Jane?" and Dylan at once shoots back, "Queen Jane is a man."[27] It is appropriate here to note that he stated in another interview that God was a woman. Reporter: "What is your belief in God? Are you a Christian?" Dylan: "Well, first of all, God is a woman. We all know that. Well, you take it from there."[28] (This was not recently.)

Talking of God and turning to the other extreme of the interpreter's art, we can note with relief that Stephen Pickering's *Bob Dylan Approximately: A Portrait of the Jewish Poet in Search of God* takes a more exalted view of our artist's preoccupations. The author interprets almost everything Dylan has ever written in the light of Jewish religious texts, and almost solely in that light, which does not strike me as a fruitful approach to the real religious content of his songs. Dylan is not, throughout most of his career, in the business of subjecting the immediate matter of life to definition in terms of any religious or philosophical system; what he does do is to allow the impingements upon his consciousness of the numinous, the other, to find expression, where that is appropriate, in religious imagery. When he *does*, in his most recent work, submit himself to an ordered set of beliefs, the expression which these find in his songs is absolutely overt and unequivocal.

Enough general remarks have been made by way of introduction. It is now time to look at the substance of Dylan's songs.

Chapter Two

How Does It Feel?

'Like a Rolling Stone' has been described as "Dylan's quintessential work",[1] and with good reason. The first line of its refrain, "How does it feel? How does it feel?", rendered by Dylan in many different versions of the song with varying emphasis and interpretation but always with rock-bottom intensity of feeling, gives us the very kernel of his art. It is the element of feeling which, in interviews, he has consistently stressed as the essence of his work, and in one he gives us a picture of himself "trying to figure out whether it was this way or that way, just what *is* it, what's the simplest way I can tell the story and make this feeling real."[2] In this process lies the key to his almost limitless emotional range, which has led many a Dylan enthusiast to remark that whatever one is feeling in any situation, Dylan has always written a song which says it all. He tells us what he feels himself, he projects himself with eerie immediacy into the feelings of others, and in so doing he shows us what *we* feel too.

This is the underlying activity of all his writing and his music-making, but nowhere is it more apparent than in that large body of songs which deal with personal relationships: not simply those which are addressed to lovers or former lovers, though there are many of those, but all which find their subject in the infinite varieties of human confrontation, which give us human beings acting upon and reacting to each other. Such songs stand at the centre of Dylan's achievement.

When Dylan talks of making a "feeling real" he does not of course mean necessarily a single, simple, indivisible feeling which can be isolated from a wider range of experience. More often the songs deal with a nucleus or complex of feelings from which may radiate tentacles which reach out towards areas connected to the centre only by the links of resonance and association. There *are* however songs, particularly some early ones, which seek no more than to communicate as faithfully as possible one emotional truth, and in some of these we can see at work, at a local level, the kind of effects which Dylan also deploys as part of a larger undertaking in more complex works. As an example of the most straightforward of these we can take 'Girl From the North Country', which is simply a tender

14

remembrance of a past love and works by means of evocation, drawing upon the universal experience of the way in which our memories of people are indelibly associated with the scenes in which we have known them. But by using the device of asking another to "Remember me to one who lives there", and to see to her well-being on his behalf, Dylan unobtrusively heightens the poignancy of the emotion by indicating at once his desire to communicate his feeling to the girl, and the impossibility of doing so in a direct way. It is a device which he was to use again years later, as we shall see.

In 'Tomorrow is a Long Time' (once recorded by Elvis Presley) the emotion to be expressed is again as simple as possible: grief at being parted from his true love. Here he indicates a subjective state of mind by means of figurative imagery, and in this very early song it is already characteristic Dylan:

> I can't see my reflection in the waters,
> I can't speak the sounds that show no pain,
> I can't hear the echo of my footsteps,
> Or can't remember the sounds of my own name.

The authenticity of the feeling is indicated in the second line by the singer's inability to achieve the conventional putting-on of a brave face. It is also worthy of note how, on the early concert version of the song released on *Greatest Hits Volume Two*, Dylan obviates the danger of mawkishness in the lines from the last verse, "But none of these and nothing else can touch the beauty / That I remember in my true love's eyes", by a sudden, unexpected hardness in his delivery of the last phrase, which takes us by surprise just as we are about to give way to a mood of sweetness. Such vocal contributions to the sense of the words are inseparable from their total "meaning", and serve as a constant reminder that Dylan's lyrics cannot be discussed without our continually maintaining in the forefront of consciousness the memory of the way – often, indeed, the alternative ways – in which Dylan delivers them.

In 'One Too Many Mornings' these approaches are combined and expanded in the communication of a feeling which is a little more complex, a little more ambiguous. The situation behind the song is not clearly defined: we know only that the lovers have parted, perhaps in acrimony, each maintaining his or her point of view. This, indeed, we learn only from the last verse: the first two are devoted to establishing that "restless hungry feeling", and we are half-way through the song before the basis of the regret is suggested by the lines "As I turn my head back to the room / Where my love and I have laid." The evocation of atmosphere is subtle:

> Down the street the dogs are barkin'

VOICE WITHOUT RESTRAINT

And the day is a-gettin' dark.
As the night comes in à-fallin',
The dogs'll lose their bark . . .

Having made use of the barking dog image in the first line, a lesser writer would probably have sought for something new to enhance the effect in the third; instead of which Dylan returns to it and extracts from it a subtler potential. The dogs don't just cease to bark but *lose* their bark. The line not only makes a recognisable feature of evening come alive in our mind's ear, but in passing says something sympathetic, strangely poignant and quite unparaphrasable about the nature of doggishness. Equally effective is the image of the silent night shattering "from the sounds inside my mind", which serves as a first specific link between the atmosphere evoked and the human drama associated with it. "The crossroads of my doorstep" at the beginning of the second verse hints at a crossroads in the relationship which is just about to be mentioned for the first time, and as the singer gazes back "to the street, / The sidewalk and the sign," we know that he does so not just from his stance at the crossroads reached at that moment summoned back from the past, but also from the longer perspective from which the song itself is sung. It is from that perspective that the last verse reaches back:

It's a restless hungry feeling
That don't mean no one no good,
When ev'rything I'm a-sayin'
You can say it just as good.
You're right from your side,
I'm right from mine.
We're both just one too many mornings
An' a thousand miles behind.

This is one of those songs in which Dylan looks back on a relationship from an attitude of "calm of mind" (though not necessarily of "all passion spent"), and with a creative effort of fairness and impartiality towards things as they are or have been. Yet it is seldom quite as simple as that. The balance of that last verse, as sung, is slightly illusory. "You're right from your side, / I'm right from mine": the two halves of that proposition look equal and congruent on the page, but in the original version of the song Dylan places slight, unobtrusive but definite emphases on the words "I'm" and "mine". This is a typical gesture of artistic honesty, recognising as it does the truth that whatever one's objective impartiality, the view from within one's own skin always finally carries the most weight.

It is interesting to compare 'One Too Many Mornings' with a

very much later song of the same type, 'If You See Her, Say Hello' from the *Blood on the Tracks* album. It too has a simple feeling to put over – in spite of everything that has passed between them he wishes her well, and he wants her to know it; and as with the songs we have been considering much of its effect comes from the beauty of its melodic line. Its method however is utterly different. Evocative imagery is almost absent, reduced to a single line in the last verse which merely gestures towards that associative resonance which was so important an element in 'One Too Many Mornings': "Sundown, yellow moon / I replay the past". Instead of building up an atmosphere and understating the story, leaving it largely to be inferred from slender hints, this song gives us a great deal of information. We learn that the girl has departed, probably for Tangier, in early spring; that the singer hasn't forgotten her in spite of their separation; that they fell out and that she made the move to end the relationship; that he desires her happiness in spite of the resultant bitterness which still "lingers on"; that he can't get her out of his head and, finally, that he would like to see her again. The device employed for telling the story is that already used in 'Girl from the North Country', the addressing of the song to a third party who is given certain simple instructions, in this case to say hello to the girl, deliver a kiss, and "Tell her she can look me up / If she's got the time." All this is achieved with the utmost economy, in five verses of eight very short lines each, and the way it is done is to make each piece of information given at once an essential link in the story, and as emotionally telling as possible without self-indulgence. Dylan is thus enabled to convey a much greater sense of complexity, of emotional subtlety in the presentment of a relationship, than in the earlier song, while at the same time giving expression to a basically uncomplicated and spontaneous *feeling*. He is expressing, again, a fully assimilated experience, so that the statements made are a thousand miles from the raw sentiments which made failures of such songs as 'I Don't Believe You' and 'Ballad in Plain D', in which Dylan first attempted to analyse the dynamics of human relationships, as opposed to giving form to an emotional deposit as in the early successes.

Part of the success of 'If You See Her' is, once more, closely bound up with the way he sings it. Cliché is the lifeblood of love songs, but if it is to be effectively used it must be cleansed of its vulgarity without in the process being stripped of its sincerity. Dylan deals with cliché in this song – and the cliché lies as much in the situation as in the words used to describe it – either by handling it in a "knowing" way, by saying "yes I know this sounds corny but I'm telling it the way it really was"; or by confronting it head-on, driving through the sentiment of the words to the base of passion which underlies them. To list the various phrases which he copes with in these ways would be valueless: the achievement is a triumph of intelligent instinct which can only be appreciated as it is heard.

It is worth noting here that all the songs we have been looking at have been what might be called after-love songs. It will be found in fact that the great majority of Dylan's love (and hate) songs come into this category. Those that deal with a happy and continuing relationship are comparatively few, nor, with one or two exceptions, are these among the most striking. This may have as much to do with the nature of love songs – and perhaps of love – as it has to do with Dylan. The habit of singing about past relationships is at any rate so inveterate that even a song like 'You're Gonna Make Me Lonesome When You Go' – a witty and light-hearted number which celebrates an on-going and possibly none too serious affair – takes its direction, as the title implies, by paradoxically looking ahead (I had better not say forward) to the time when the lover addressed will be gone.

Many of the songs which have been described as "put-downs" are really aiming at a mood of emotional realism. Jon Landau, after condemning 'Don't Think Twice, It's All Right' as an unsympathetic, unsubtle and one-dimensional put-down, is forced to concede that "the beauty of Dylan's vocal-guitar-harmonica performance doesn't really say what the words do and, in fact, really transforms the verbal meaning of the song into something much deeper and much less coarse".[3] The point must be repeated that the "meaning" of a Dylan song is *not* necessarily just what the words say (though they may make the predominant contribution), and indeed may depend for its realisation precisely on tensions between the words and the other elements involved; but that apart, it does not seem to me that the words of 'Don't Think Twice' have the unsympathetic qualities which Landau attributes to them. The feeling that is being aimed at is a balanced reconciliation between a sense of hurt and a realistic understanding, and the rather flip tone serves as a defence against the hurt suffered, which is more than hinted at in lines like "Still I wish there was something you would do or say / To try and make me change my mind and stay"; and "It ain't no use in callin' out my name, gal / Like you never did before"; and "I ain't sayin' you treated me unkind / You could have done better but I don't mind". The attitude of defence is itself, of course, part of the feeling which Dylan is trying to "make real". The effort to sympathise with the girl's point of view is not easy, and in the lines in which he tries hardest to do so – recognising that this woman is emotionally a child – he switches, in order to make objectivity easier, from addressing her as "you" to referring to her in the third person:

HOW DOES IT FEEL?

I'm a—thinkin' and a-wonderin' all the way down the road
I once loved a woman, a child I'm told
I give her my heart but she wanted my soul
But don't think twice, it's all right.

The return to the direct address in the refrain is in that context a
return to outgoing human sympathy, even though a doubt remains
as to whether it really is as "all right" as he claims. (That doubt is
underlined in the *Budokan* version, in which at the end of the song
Dylan repeats the phrase again and again in a variety of conflicting
intonations, ending with a particularly flat, drawn-out kind of
howl.)

There are a number of songs of the period up to *Blonde on Blonde*
which present, with varying degrees of irony and from differing
vantage points, such a "sane man's view" of finished, dying or
unpromising relationships. Several are valedictory, like 'It Ain't
Me, Babe' and 'It's All Over Now, Baby Blue', offering probably
unwelcome but certainly sound advice as a parting gift. 'It Ain't
Me, Babe' is a warning-off song, aimed at discouraging a starry-
eyed admirer, while "Baby Blue" advises a dismissed lover to put
the past behind her (or, as we are confidently informed by a number
of commentators, him) and "start anew". There is certainly an
element of hardness in these songs which can look like cruelty:

Go melt back into the night, babe,
Everything inside is made of stone.
There's nothing in here moving
An' anyway I'm not alone.

In "Baby Blue" Dylan gets into the skin of the person whose world
is breaking up with vertiginous images like "the sky, too, is folding
under you", and "The carpet, too, is moving under you". This
implacable quality should however be seen as part of the effort
towards emotional realism. In neither song is Dylan putting
someone down; rather he is advising them to "think positively", in a
way which implies a genuine concern:

Leave your stepping stones behind, something calls for you.
Forget the dead you've left, they will not follow you.
The vagabond who's knocking at your door
Is standing in the clothes that you once wore.
Strike another match, go start anew
And it's all over now, Baby Blue.

'One of Us Must Know (Sooner or Later)' is a post-mortem song in
which Dylan admits a sense of his own fault in ways which are

subtler than might at first appear:

> I didn't mean to treat you so bad
> You shouldn't take it so personal
> I didn't mean to make you so sad
> You just happened to be there, that's all.

The apparent naïveté of the approach is undercut by the singing: clearly he understands very well that it was entirely natural that she should "take it so personal", while the fourth line implicitly confesses to the unthinking egotism with which he has treated her. Against this is balanced the evident sincerity with which he sings each time the last line of the refrain: "That I really *did* try to get close to you."

But there *are* of course songs which deal with people in a very much harsher idiom. A group in particular springs to mind from the time of *Highway 61 Revisited* – 'Like a Rolling Stone', 'Queen Jane Approximately', 'Ballad of a Thin Man' and 'Positively 4th Street'. A remark which Dylan made to Anthony Scaduto may be mentioned here. "I discovered that when I used words like 'he' or 'it' or 'they' and talking about other people, I was really talking about nobody but me," he said. ". . . You see, I hadn't really known before, that I was writing about myself in all those songs."[4] This interesting comment has been taken in an absurdly literal way by several writers on Dylan, leading Craig McGregor, for instance, to conjecture that Queen Jane may be "Dylan himself".[5] Actually, of course, it is quite impossible to write a song "about" oneself, in a literal sense, and remain unaware of it. What Dylan was talking about was surely what Keats called "negative capability", the capacity of certain kinds of sensibility to imagine the experience of others *as if* it were their own, to enter, for the time being, another personality, and to project one's own experience into one's understanding of another's. It relates, too, to the words of Dylan's master Rimbaud, *Je est un autre*.' Dylan possesses to an exceptional degree the quality of imaginative empathy, and it is just this which in a strange way humanises his most bitter and corrosive attacks. By entering the skin of his "victims" he ensures that he does not treat them as mere objects, he acknowledges their common humanity. So when, with terrifying exultation, he intones "How does it fee-eel? How does it fee-ee-eel?" we know that he understands, himself, just how it must feel.

Such an understanding always implies a degree of sympathy. This is borne out by a marvellous line in 'Queen Jane Approximately'. Throughout most of this song Dylan appears to be revelling in the discomfiture which he envisages Queen Jane as experiencing in the future, and it sounds as if, when he sings "Won't you come see me, Queen Jane?'', he is looking forward to crowing over her plight. Then, in the last verse, comes the line "And you want someone you don't have to speak to", and we see that he has another motive in making his plea – he sees himself as offering that unvocal sympathy which, perhaps, "negative capability" alone can provide. In fact, both motives are probably present: he does want to crow too, but in the last analysis the more generous impulse takes pride of place. There is always, too, with Dylan the feeling that all positions are potentially reversible. This sense is expressed in the ending of 'To Ramona':

> And someday maybe,
> Who knows, baby,
> I'll come and be cryin' to you.

The further import of Dylan's remark to Scaduto relates to his fundamental purpose in writing all his songs – to get to the truth of a feeling. The feelings in question are generally his own, and in that sense the songs may be said to be about himself. But those feelings are nonetheless usually concerned with other people. Often the emotions expressed are quite primitive: they can be far removed from the balanced, objective summings-up to which some of the songs we discussed earlier were devoted. To complain that a song like 'Positively 4th Street' is "bitter" is to present Dylan with no case to answer. To give expression to the feeling of undiluted, remorseless bitterness – something which a good many people must have experienced at times – is precisely its purpose. By its success in conveying that feeling it adds to the repertoire of the emotions which have been realised and sublimated in art. (And to see how little this repertoire is increased by an attempt which fails we need look no further than 'Ballad in Plain D.')

'Like a Rolling Stone' seems to be one of a pair with 'Queen Jane Approximately' – Dylan goes in for matching or contrasting pairs of songs on several of his albums. What is envisaged in 'Queen Jane' seems, in 'Like a Rolling Stone', to have happened, and Dylan is now crowing. The "jugglers and the clowns" who frown when they do "tricks for you" could indeed be the same clowns that Queen Jane "commissioned." From the first lines he seems to be rubbing her face in it:

> Once upon a time you dressed so fine
> You threw the bums a dime in your prime, didn't you?

That taunt gives the tone of the song: he wants her to admit that she is down and out. He piles up images that suggest a person success-ful, extraverted and full of confidence (if somewhat unaware), only to reveal her feet of clay. Yet if ever there was a case of the total sense of a Dylan song springing from much more than the words, and of the other elements modifying the verbal meaning, it must be this. The song has had a lot of attention and I don't want to comment on it at length; but its greatness lies in its capacity to expand and take on new resonances and emotional tones, and this it owes largely to its magnificent, celebratory, affirmative melody. After the hard confidence of the original treatment, and the Dionysiac exultation of the version on *Before the Flood*, it becomes, on the *Budokan* album, a profoundly sad, wise and sympathetic piece, closer in mood to what is expressed in the last lines of that wonderfully tender and evocative song, 'It Takes a Lot to Laugh, It Takes a Train to Cry':

> Well, I wanna be your lover, baby,
> I don't wanna be your boss.
> Don't say I never warned you
> When your train gets lost.

'Like a Rolling Stone' is a work which grows and matures in as moving and unexpected ways as does the man who wrote it. (And shrinks, also, with his temporary retreats: it is rather poignant to hear that pulsing rhythm held in unnatural restraint so as to accommodate the stubbornly tame interpretation which Dylan gives us on the Isle of Wight track included in *Self Portrait* – so tame and so reductive of the song's real mood that in the words "How does it feel?" he even puts almost as strong an emphasis on "does" as on "feel".)

'Positively 4th Street' has no such potential breadth of sympathy but it does have its own prickly integrity. It is an extremely tightly constructed song with an unending, circular musical pattern, each verse formally corresponding to one musical unit but the variable rhyme scheme being based on two, which allows for some neat effects making use of matching verses. The jaunty, carefree tune – we can picture Dylan strolling whistling down 4th Street, hands in pockets – ironically offsets the pitiless, clinical exposure of hypocrisy which is the song's unrelenting business. It is probably addressed to some friend who has let Dylan down; but in the one verse where "he" is referred to in the printed text, "it" is substituted in the song as sung:

> Do you take me for such a fool
> To think I'd make contact
> With the one who tries to hide
> What it don't know to begin with

The purpose of this could be to leave the person's sex indeterminate, but more likely it is to reduce his status to that of an object. This does not, I think, contradict my earlier contention that Dylan humanises his attacks on his victims by putting himself in their position; for he is calling the person "it" here for a conscious purpose of invective and not out of a failure of imaginative sympathy. Indeed his innate tendency to put himself in the other person's shoes is here made literal, again with a polemical object in view, in what must be the ultimate in gestures of rejection:

> I wish that for just one time
> You could stand inside my shoes
> And just for that one moment
> I could be you
>
> Yes, I wish that for just one time
> You could stand inside my shoes
> You'd know what a drag it is
> To see you

The refined cruelty of this is remarkable. The repetition of the proposition keeps the listener in suspense, perhaps hoping for a more sympathetic line than the song has so far displayed; for the wish that the other "could stand inside my shoes" might be expected to mean "understand my point of view" rather than what it does mean, "see you as I do"; and in the light of that expectation "And just for that one moment / I could be you" could even seem to express an outgoing impulse instead of the sneer which it later proves to be. The "feeling" behind the whole song is perfectly embodied in those last lines and the way Dylan sings them; and to have allowed any element of charity to creep in would have been to be untrue to the feeling which grows out of the first verse:

> You got a lotta nerve
> To say you are my friend
> When I was down
> You just stood there grinning

'Ballad of a Thin Man' is a song which has been subjected to a profusion of interpretations. I have seen Mr Jones confidently identified as variously a newspaper reporter, a "representative of the unhip world", "the respectable man in the street and probably you and I", "the pop equivalent of Mr Charlie", and Bob Dylan. Dylan has said that he is "a fella that came into a truck-stop once." It is also suggested (by Craig McGregor, Michael Gray and others) that the situation in which Mr Jones is lost involves a homosexual propositioning. None of this really matters: what matters is that he is someone – anyone – who finds himself vulnerable, exposed and alone in a situation which he does not understand and cannot control:

> You raise up your head
> And you ask, "Is this where it is?"
> And somebody points to you and says
> "It's his"
> And you say "What's mine?"
> And somebody else says "Where what is?"
> And you say, "Oh my God
> Am I here all alone?"

The helplessness, the confusion, the feeling that you are being laughed at and that whatever you say next will be wrong – everyone must at some time or another have felt something like this and said to himself "Oh my God / Am I here all alone?" Mr Jones is observed from the outside but we are obliged to feel with him because we know no more about what is "happening here" than he does; the story is told from an implied position of omniscience which we are not permitted to share – Dylan understands what it's all about, we feel, but we don't, any more than Mr Jones does (which is why we feel obliged to attempt an interpretation). He is being mocked, but we are not able to go comfortably along with the mockery because the victim is too close to ourselves. That Dylan is able to bring off such an effect is, of course, dependent on his own act of empathy.

There is a passage in the section of *Tarantula* called "Sand in the Mouth of the Movie Star"[6] which seems closely related to 'Ballad of a Thin Man' (both belong to roughly the same period). It is worth looking at as an illustration of how Dylan seems to need the disciplines of song writing to define and direct his insights. The prose passage is unfocused, diffuse and lacking in impact, and would probably go unremarked without a knowledge of the song, which provides a clue to what the writer is driving at. It would be interesting to know which came first; most likely the prose contains the germ of the song.

We have been looking at songs which appear to be mainly negative in attitude. But the point is really – and this is something that will crop up again and again – that Dylan is one of those artists who most often define their *values* negatively – in terms of what they are against rather than of what they are for. This can be clearly seen in a song which has a very positive outlook and tone – 'All I Really Want to Do.' This is one of the wittiest and most high-spirited of the early songs, very sharp psychologically, full of nimble internal rhyming, and delivered in a chuckling, irreverent, half-mocking but very engaging tone of voice. The whole song is devoted to a catalogue of the things Dylan *doesn't* want to do to the girl, set only against the recurrent protestation: "All I really want to do / Is, baby, be friends with you." This disclaimer is, of course, tinged with irony, for whatever he may *not* want to do it is certain that he is interested in being more than just "friends" with her. But the phrase points effectively to a straight-forward and uncomplicated attitude which stands in contrast to the kind of intense, soul-searching approach to sexual relationships which is what he is satirising – what D. H. Lawrence used to call "sex-in-the-head":

> I ain't lookin' to block you up,
> Shock or knock or lock you up,
> Analyse you, categorize you,
> Finalize you or advertise you.

The picture that is built up of the woman he is addressing is of one who likes to accuse her lover of such objectives precisely because she herself is stuck firmly in her head. Against this claustrophobic cerebral closeness Dylan asserts his own self-sufficient singleness:

> I ain't lookin' for you to feel like me,
> See like me or be like me.

This is a perennial Dylan theme. We find it again in 'Maggie's Farm':

> Well, I try my best
> To be just like I am,
> But everybody wants you
> To be just like them.

It crops up once more as late as the *Slow Train Coming* album, in 'I Believe in You', where his friends show him the door "'cause I don't be like they'd like me to".

What Dylan is saying in 'All I Really Want to Do' is entirely positive in spirit, but it is highly characteristic of him that it is presented in a negative form. The lover who receives perhaps his highest and most finely-wrought praise – the woman of 'Love Minus Zero / No Limit' – has attributes which are formulated either negatively or by means of such suggestive paradoxes as are used to describe spiritual things in the language used by Eastern religion. Thus "she speaks like silence, / Without ideals or violence", "she laughs like the flowers"; her insights and attitudes belong to the spirit of Zen:

> She knows there's no success like failure
> And that failure's no success at all.
> . . . . .
> My love winks, she does not bother,
> She knows too much to argue or to judge.

The values represented by this lover are defined in contrast to the ways of the world – the insincere gestures, the lost and futile talk, the insubstantiality of material things, the confused spiritual strivings – all suggested in marvellously rich and concrete language. The positive values find their place within a harsh, elemental world:

> The wind howls like a hammer
> The wind blows cold and rainy,
> My love she's like some raven
> At my window with a broken wing.

The "broken wing" is one of those flashes of imaginative insight which only a great artist can make livingly concrete. It comes as a surprise, for all the previous imagery has suggested someone secure, confident, untouched, almost remote, standing above the common exigencies of living by virtue of spiritual strangths; but when the image comes it impels our assent, for with its suggestion of vulnerability-within-strength it establishes her humanity: this is no goddess and no abstraction, but a woman who lives out her values in the world. (The image also of course conjures up the austerity of Poe's Raven which knocks at his chamber-door to deliver its laconic message "Nevermore". A skein of probably unconscious associations may have been at work to contribute to the imagery of this verse. The "country doctor" who appears in the second line comes from Kafka's story of that name; "Kafka" in Czech means raven or jackdaw, and such a bird was the emblem of the Kafka family business; also, Kafka is said to have seen a bird of evil omen – I think an owl – at his window on the night before his death. Could a train of association have led Dylan from Kafka to the Raven of Poe's poem?)

'She Belongs To Me' has sometimes been taken for a similar hymn of praise, but it does not appear so to me. It does seem to make a pair with 'Love Minus Zero', but such pairings among Dylan's songs generally imply some degree of contrast. The irony surely begins with the title, for it could much more aptly be called "I Belong To Her", and the song is almost as much about what it feels like to belong to her as it is about the woman herself. Her dominance is complete: she is self-centred, imperious, probably capricious, certainly predatory. The singer's thraldom is such that his lover colours the very texture of his days and nights:

> She can take the dark out of the nighttime
> And paint the daytime black.

This woman too has a certain spiritual power, or power of personality, but unlike the other she uses it to dominate and to feed her ego:

HOW DOES IT FEEL?

You will start out standing
Proud to steal her anything she sees.
But you will end up peeking through her keyhole
Down upon your knees.

(Dylan admits this as his own experience implicitly, through the title.) Again, unlike the other, she appears invulnerable, untouchable in a way which seems only doubtfully a compliment:

She never stumbles,
She's got no place to fall.
She's nobody's child,
The law can't touch her at all.

The basis of the relationship is succinctly summed up in the lines "She's a hypnotist collector, / You are a walking antique"; and when Dylan suggests buying her a trumpet for Halloween, we are left wondering whether this is so that she can blow her own. The mood of the song is of a kind of despairing admiration for the enormity of it all. But of course it is not an objective summing-up of an actual woman: it is a putting-out-there of a specific feeling. It is even possible that the women of the two songs are actually one, seen from the vantage-point of different feeelings, of different motions of the will. James Joyce attributes to Shem the Penman in *Finnegans Wake* the two complementary functions of the artist: "He points the deathbone and the quick are still . . . He lifts the lifewand and the dumb speak." If in 'Love Minus Zero' Dylan lifts the lifewand, 'She Belongs To Me' is one of the songs in which he points the deathbone.

2

With 'Visions of Johanna' we come to a very much richer and more complex song, one of Dylan's greatest achievements and, for me at least, the summation of that stage of his development which culminates in *Blonde on Blonde*. Michael Gray has shown[7] how favourably it compares with the other long song on the album, 'Sad-Eyed Lady of the Lowlands', in spite of the latter's having much more the air of being self-consciously a set-piece. The construction of the lyrics in relation to the music is of absorbing interest in 'Visions of Johanna', but that aspect can most conveniently be discussed in a later chapter. I want here to examine the thematic development of the song as it is evolved through the imagery.

'Visions of Johanna' centres on a counterpoint between two love-relationships, one past and one present, and the conflicting values which they represent. Johanna is noteworthy by her continued physical absence throughout the song and her overwhelming psychic presence, while Louise is very much in the forefront of what

27

action there is. All the characters play different roles at various moments within the shifting dreamlike scenes that pass before our eyes: Johanna can probably be identified with the Mona Lisa of the fourth verse and with the Madonna figure of the last, in which Louise seems to play the part of "The countess who's pretending to care for him". The third element of the triangle, the "I" figure, undergoes an even more bewildering series of transformations, appearing variously as Louise's lover, "little boy lost", the peddler, perhaps also the fiddler, "you", and of course the straightforward first person singular. This fragmentation of his own personality (if we can dare to make that assumption) into projections of its different aspects or functions, allows Dylan to subject himself to a far subtler and more complex self-criticism than he has previously attempted; and it also reflects the nature of the song's imagery which, as with so many Dylan songs and most obviously so at this period, forms a mosaic of discrete impressions and colours which, seen in perspective, blend to create a whole and self-consistent world of the senses.

The first line evokes an atmosphere which the ensuing verse proceeds to make concrete: "Ain't it just like the night to play tricks when you're trying to be so quiet?" We see with solid clarity the lovers in the room, Louise holding "a handful of rain" (which in this case probably *does* mean heroin), "temptin' you to defy it", the flickering lights from across the street, hear the coughing heat-pipes and the country music station playing soft background music; and experience withal an odd sense of emptiness, lack of purpose, called up by the second line, "We sit here stranded, though we're all doing our best to deny it". The presence of the narrator is announced by that "we", and the fragmentation of the actors by the word "all", for we are about to learn that there are in fact only two people in the room:

> Just Louise and her lover so entwined
> And these visions of Johanna that conquer my mind.

Just as Johanna is physically absent but vastly present in "my mind", so the singer is physically present but psychically absent – the last line of the next verse makes that explicit: "Where these visions of Johanna have now taken my place." This second verse begins by taking us out to the world of night beyond the warmth of the room where the lovers lie entwined – a surreal night which causes the night watchman to click his flashlight in alarm. Within, the narrator is protected:

> Louise, she's all right, she's just near
> She's delicate and seems like the mirror
> But she just makes it all too concise and too clear

HOW DOES IT FEEL?

That Johanna's not here
The ghost of 'lectricity howls in the bones of her face
  Where these visions of Johanna have now taken my place.

So though protected he is not satisfied, and with that extraordinary metaphor of the fifth line, which so finely exemplifies Baudelaire's theory of *correspondances* and might well have been envied by the Rimbaud of the sonnet 'Voyelles', we explicitly learn why: even as he lies in the arms of Louise his thoughts are with his former love.

  This theme is further developed in the next verse, the verse of the "little boy lost":

Now, little boy lost, he takes himself so seriously
He brags of his misery, he likes to live dangerously
And when bringing her name up
He speaks of a farewell kiss to me
He's sure got a lotta gall to be so useless and all
Muttering small talk at the wall while I'm in the hall . . .

The cluster of character traists projected in the image of the little boy lost is delineated with remarkable economy in these lines: the passivity expressed in the weak feminine rhymes "seriously" and "dangerously" (both sung by Dylan with self-deprecating irony); the element of exhibitionism and self-indulgence shown up in "brags of his misery" and the drawn-out parody of feeling of "a farewell kiss to me" (the lack of inverted commas around the phrase perhaps throwing out a hint that we are permitted to identify him with the "I" figure); the blatancy of those piled-up internal rhymes – gall, all, small talk, wall, hall – somehow embodying the effrontery of the little boy's hypocrisy. For undoubtedly he is bragging of his misery over the loss of one even as he makes love to another – "in the hall" with Dylan is a metaphor for the sexual act or its imminence. The extravagant mocking emphasis that Dylan places on that "*I'*m" when he sings it surely underlines the actual identity of "he" and "I" while overtly denying it. The ineffectiveness of the character's self-dramatising, above all, is comically brought out by the deft phrase "gall to be so useless". In all this Dylan's use of his voice is at its most supply intelligent, working along with the words to draw a psychological thumb-nail portrait which is completely convincing. And the whole is strangely authenticated by the lines which follow, which acknowledge the valid feeling which underlies all the posturing which has just been sent up:

How can I explain?
Oh, it's so hard to get on
And these visions of Johanna, they kept me up past the dawn.

The fourth verse changes the scene with another kaleidoscopic flash, and we find ourselves inside the museums where "Infinity goes up on trial". The presence of Mona Lisa tells us, I think, why this scene is introduced. As we envisage the famous painting hanging on the wall of the Louvre with its celebrated enigmatic smile – here attributed, in a notorious drug reference, to "the highway blues" – we are being told something about what Johanna represents to the singer. For Mona Lisa is a madonna, a mother-figure, but also one who is remote, apart and inscrutable, and in her position of honour on the museum wall stuck up, as it were, on a pedestal, taken out of life. This is the first hint offered that these "visions of Johanna" are more ambiguous than we might have supposed: they are not the straightforward fructifying influence that we might imagine. Infinity is going "up on trial" here, "salvation" is associated with the monotony and the lifelessness of the fixed and permanent; and I think that Johanna is being linked with these values that are coming under critical scrutiny. The lines which follow can be read in a way which accords with this suspicion:

> See the primitive wall flower freeze
> When the jelly-faced women all sneeze
> Hear the one with the mustache say "Jeeze
> I can't find my knees"
> Oh, jewels and binoculars hang from the head of the mule
> But these visions of Johanna, they make it all seem so cruel.

The type of vision encapsulated in these lines is typical of the Dylan of such songs as 'Stuck Inside of Mobile', 'Just Like Tom Thumb's Blues', and 'Desolation Row', and I suspect that they are intended as a kind of summing-up, almost a parody, of that kind of vision, whose drug links are probably made explicit by their proximity to that phrase "the highway blues". Why they might "seem so cruel" is obvious enough; but the word "seem", I believe, is the operative one here. When he sings that word Dylan gives it a slight, definite emphasis, such as we found him imparting to the words "I'm" and "mine" in 'One Too Many Mornings'. By doing so he stays loyal to his own vision even while celebrating – or seeming to celebrate – the counter-vision, counter-value, represented by Johanna.

The new personnel introduced in the final verse correspond to a further projection of an aspect of the character of the "I" figure. The persona of the peddler gives us the acerbic, cynical, misanthropic Dylan, and also his longest-ever line: "Sayin', 'Name me someone that's not a parasite and I'll go out and say a prayer for him.'" This is answered, not directly, by the habitual saying of Louise: "Ya can't look at much, can ya man?" The coarseness of this represents a tit-for-tat in terms of cynicism; and the following line, "As she, herself, prepares for him", suggests an element of hyprocrisy in Louise's character which corresponds to that exhibited by little boy lost. This reinforces the impression given by the countess's "pretending to care for him", although the identity between the two is not made explicit. The focus now switches once more to Johanna:

> And Madonna, she still has not showed
> We see this empty cage now corrode
> Where her cape of the stage once had flowed
> The fiddler, he now steps to the road
> He writes ev'rything's been returned which was owed
> On the back of the fish truck that loads
> While my conscience explodes . . .

The imagery is again strongly visual here: we can see the rusting, corroding bars of the empty cage, representing the sterility of regret in which the singer is imprisoned, and contrasting with the richness and flowing movement of Madonna's "cape of the stage"; and we can see the fiddler licking his finger like a schoolboy before scrawling his message in the dirt on the back of the fish truck. But the most striking feature of the verse is the succession of seven rhyming lines (there have been only four in the equivalent places in the previous verses) which culminate in "my conscience explodes". The first six are sung to the same repeated musical line, and the process mimics the build-up, the accumulation of held-down energy, which leads up to a physical explosion; while the slight variation provided by the "s" of "loads" and "explodes" saves the device from monotony. It is one of Dylan's most effective enactments of his meaning. Following on this tour-de-force he throws in another inspired, instinctual image that registers directly on our nerves, and brings the song to rest with swift but measured calm:

> The harmonicas play the skeleton keys and the rain
> And these visions of Johanna are now all that remain.

I said at the beginning of my discussion that this song had to do with a contrapuntal treatment of the values represented by two lovers. If, as I have tried to show, the visions aroused by Johanna are not as wholly positive as their dominance might lead us to suppose, nor are the feelings centred on Louise as negative as those references in the final verse suggest. Throughout the song she seems to stand for a sometimes harsh but at bottom caring realism, as opposed to the more exalted but perhaps less substantial state of consciousness associated with Johanna. If the "rain" of verse one is indeed heroin, Louise's gesture in "temptin' you to defy it" seems positive. In the second verse she appears in a reassuring role, contrasted with the risks and wiles of the night outside, and described in a way which suggests an understated but sincere compliment. Her function as a mirror-image of the singer – "She's delicate and seems like the mirror" – reappears in a different way in the last verse where she trades street-wisdom with the peddler; her part there is to recall him to a sense of objectivity. As so often with Dylan, the differing values embodied in Johanna and Louise are held, in the overall vision of the song, in a state of delicate equilibrium.

3

Blonde on Blonde ends a major period in which Dylan not only felt intensely about the varieties of human relationships but was ready to transmute these feelings into art. After the gap in his activity which followed his motor cycle accident late in 1966, a change is immediately evident. Insofar as they deal with such things at all, the songs of the *Basement Tapes* period confront love and sex in a spirit of cynicism and often from an obscene angle. Many of them – ditties like 'Please, Mrs Henry', 'Tiny Montgomery', 'Million Dollar Bash' and 'Apple Suckling Tree' – are simply exercises in innuendo, and the sexuality which they celebrate is generally perverted in one direction or another. They are witty, adroit, and not to be taken too seriously. Dylan and The Band sound as if they were having a lot of fun with them – there is a moment for instance in 'Please, Mrs Henry' when Dylan misses a "please" because he has obviously been overtaken by laughter. They lay no claim whatever to depth or complexity, nor is there any reason why they should. (There are of course serious songs in this series, but their preoccupations are quite different.) And in the one song of dismissal on the *Basement Tapes* album – 'Down in the Flood' – Dylan perhaps comes as close as he does anywhere to a straightforward put-down:

> Oh, mama, ain't you gonna miss your best friend now?
> Yes, you're gonna have to find yourself
> Another best friend, somehow.

In *John Wesley Harding* Dylan is ploughing another furrow altogether, and it is only in the last couple of songs – 'Down Along the Cove' and 'I'll Be your Baby Tonight' – that the love theme reappears. These songs will be looked at in a different context at a later stage; suffice it to say here that the mood in which love is approached is a radically new one for Dylan:

> Well, that mockingbird's gonna sail away,
> We're gonna forget it.
> That big fat moon's gonna shine like a spoon,
> But we're gonna let it,

HOW DOES IT FEEL?

You won't regret it . . .

Dylan had seemed to claim before, in 'All I Really Want to Do', that love was simple, but something in his jokey tone of voice in that song told us that he did not really believe it himself. Now, if he does not *really* believe it in the depths of him even yet, he seems genuinely to be trying to persuade *himself* that he believes it. Before we pass on to *Nashville Skyline*, however, not that curious "But" at the beginning of the fourth line I have just quoted.

Dylan has said in an interview that, "on *Nashville Skyline* you had to read between the lines".[8] Taking up that hint we might start at the beginning of the first song:

> To be alone with you
> Just you and me
> Now won't you tell me true
> Ain't that the way it oughta be?

That question-mark can be taken as being eloquent. It seems to represent an acknowledgement that Dylan is here *willing* himself to take up a position which he does not really *feel*; and as we have already seen, authenticity of feeling forms the stated basis of his art, without which nothing serious is possible. The position – as opposed to the feeling – which he has decided to adopt on this album is fairly given by these lines from the second song, "I Threw It All Away":

> Love is all there is, it makes the world go 'round,
> Love and only love, it can't be denied.

The question-mark is only implied this time: can't it be denied? In song number three we find a similar implication:

> Peggy Day stole my heart away
> By golly, what more can I say . . .

There seems, unfortunately, to be little more that he *can* say on *Nashville Skyline*. The most authentic song on the album is 'Lay Lady Lay', because it doesn't purport to deal with "love" so much as with desire, and with the resolution to "have your cake and eat it too". There is no reason to decry this group of songs: they are an entertaining exercise in the country style, and not an uncritical one, being far from lacking in irreverent irony. The Dylan on whom Little Jack Horner had nothing ('Country Pie') was no doubt taking a rest from himself, a temporary and necessary refuge from too much intensity, and producing some witty and enjoyable music in the process, and who should complain? Nonetheless there must at the time have been many Dylan fans who might have echoed their

33

hero as he sang:

> All of those awful things that I have heard,
> I don't want to believe them, all I want is your word.
> So darlin', I'm countin' on you,
> Tell me that it isn't true.

(A similar emotion, caused by a very different kind of development, has been abroad in 1979–80 with the issue of *Slow Train Coming* – and, I think, with less justification.) *Nashville Skyline,* at any rate, saw Dylan throwing his "troubles out the door", as he put it in 'Tonight I'll be Staying Here with You'; convinced, or attempting to be, that, "I don't need them any more." The attempt failed: " – it just went down, down, down", says Dylan in the same part of the interview already quoted. "I couldn't be anybody but myself, and at that point I didn't know it or want to know it." *Self Portrait*, like its predecessor, has much on it that is worth listening to – almost anything Dylan does has some value – but it is thin and anaemic stuff compared with what had been and what was yet to come.

> The best must be yet to come,
> That's what they explain to me . . .

So sang Dylan in 'If Dogs Run Free' on the *New Morning* album. *New Morning* is the beginning of the end of an old mood rather than the beginning of a new one. Songs like the title number and 'If Not for You' are still determinedly uncomplicated, sunny, and sincere. The record continues the pursuit of his substitute faith, and the image of Dylan as the happy family man, living a life close to nature with wife and lots of kids in the simple countryside, is projected with a tenacity which led Michael Gray to wonder (although he rightly saw certain clear signs for hope) whether, "It may even be not unduly pessimistic to suggest that Dylan has lost control over this latest (and most irritating) persona",[9] having little to say and even exhibiting a degree of complacency in the saying of that little. At moments, in fact, he gives the impression that he has now settled so comfortably into his "simple family man" image that genuine feeling may be becoming possible within its limits. Yet the same kind of questions can be read for instance between the lines of this, from 'Sign on the Window', as we surmised for some of the *Nashville Skyline* songs:

> Build me a cabin in Utah,
> Marry me a wife, catch rainbow trout,
> Have a bunch of kids who call me "Pa",
> That must be what it's all about,
> That must be what it's all about.

That repetition, as Gray points out, sounds like a farther attempt to persuade himself of what he doesn't actually feel. Only in 'The Man in Me' does he place one tentative foot on a trail which might lead him into territory where the country ethic does not hold:

The man in me will hide sometimes to keep from bein' seen,
But that's just because he doen't want to turn into some machine.

Three and a half years separate *New Morning* from *Planet Waves*; much the longest gap in Dylan's recording activity, if we ignore the soundtrack for *Pat Garrett and Billy the Kid*. In that time a fundamental change seems to have taken place, for in the new album Dylan is allowing himself to feel again. *Planet Waves* (1974) is exciting musically, and in certain songs a passion asserts itself which triumphs over lyrics which, when seen in cold print, at moments approach banality. 'Forever Young', in particular, is a song which owes its power almost entirely to passion, for the words are a mere compendium of conventional blessings. Yet the brooding intensity of the slow version on the album, and the soaring cadences of some later treatments – notably that on *Budokan* – leave us in no doubt as to its importance for Dylan. On *Planet Waves* things are stirring, still in a state of flux. The set of values which, as Michael Gray has shown, [10] *New Morning* queried and scrutinised even while asserting them, is both affirmed and undermined. The elements of doubt and affirmation set up a creative tension which is expressed most obviously in the two versions of 'Forever Young' which respectively end the first side and begin the second: the one slow and sombre, the other swift, confident and energetic. The general tendency of the record is to dispose of the doubts first and then pass on to the affirmation, and it ends with a set of powerful, almost ecstatic songs which celebrate fulfilled love, and do so with a vigour and definiteness quite different from the relaxed treatment of the subject from *Nashville Skyline* to *New Morning*. I shall approach things the other way round and glance at the "positive" songs first, as it is the others which point onwards towards the developments of *Blood on the Tracks*.

There is one very positive song on the first side – 'On a Night Like This', which starts the record off: with 'Lay Lady Lay' it is perhaps the closest Dylan approaches to evoking pure sensuality. When he sings "And let it burn, burn, burn, burn / On a night like this" it is his sheer verve and enthusiasm that tell us that he is referring to more than a log fire. A similar repetition speaks of a like full-bloodedness in another very simple song, 'You Angel You': "If this is love then gimme more / And more and more and more and more." Perhaps a clue to the changes Dylan was going through at this time is to be found in the first lines of 'Wedding Song':

VOICE WITHOUT RESTRAINT

> I love you more than ever
> More than time and more than love...

In the songs of the country period it was the abstraction, the *idea* of love with which he was concerned: he reminded himself constantly that love *ought* to be the one object of his pursuit, but very little sense of its reality was coming through. Now, he seems to be saying, he has discovered that the real thing is more important than the abstract ideal: he loves his woman more than he loves love. For the first time in years he is again singing to express things that are real to his feelings. 'Wedding Song' itself, however, is not perhaps the best example of this development. For all its exuberant rhythmic drive and its apparent confidence it is curiously one-dimensional, over-insistent and overstated:

> My thoughts of you don't ever rest
> They'd kill me if I lie
> I'd sacrifice the world for you
> And watch my senses die...

One is reminded strongly here of the competetive vying of King Lear's elder daughters in exaggerated protestations of boundless, irrational love for their father, and of Cordelia's dissenting, "I'm sure my love's / More richer than my tongue." Is it only the hindsight afforded by *Blood on the Tracks* (and, it must be admitted, events in Dylan's private life) that suggest that his confidence in 'Wedding Song' is an expression of an act of will, a determination to believe what he wants to believe? Certainly the positioning of the track at the end of the album gives an impression of papering over the cracks, attempting to dispel from our minds the sense of restlessness and foreboding set up by some of the other songs.

A far more successful and moving song, to my mind, is the much less obtrusive 'Never Say Goodbye'. For some reason I associate it in my mind with 'It Takes a Lot to Laugh, It Takes a Train to Cry.' Both have the same atmosphere of wintry beauty, the same tension between tenderness and realism, while the strength and sensitivity of the music seem to arise from and express the same type of feeling. Dylan's ability to evoke a scene in a few strokes is at its most effective (and affecting):

> Twilight on the frozen lake
> North wind about to break
> On footprints in the snow
> Silence down below.

Within its small compass it is also more complex, in terms of feeling, than either 'Wedding Song' or anything on the three previous albums. Dylan is, for one thing, prepared to acknowledge once more some degree of complexity in himself:

> My dreams are made of iron and steel
> With a big bouquet of roses hanging down
> From the heavens to the ground.

In contrast to the rather bludgeoning statements in 'Wedding Song' of the importance to him of his woman, a certain sense of dependency and uncertainty is here much more delicately suggested by a little scene which is made vivid to our mental eye:

> The crashing waves roll over me
> As I stand upon the sand
> Wait for you to come
> And grab hold of my hand.

It will also be seen from this song that Dylan's interest in imagery has undergone something of a renaissance. This is perhaps most obvious in the terse poetry of 'Tough Mama', a very interesting and underrated song which seems to be addressed to his Muse, the "Sweet Goddess / Born of a blinding light and a changing wind" whom he invokes and to whom he offers a ring. "It's my duty / To bring you down to the field where the flowers bloom" he sings; "Sweet Goddess / It must be time to carve another notch". The song expresses, in a series of fractured but very powerful images, his sense of dissatisfaction and his determination to do something about it. Similar restless, hungry feelings are communicated in simpler language in *Going, Going, Gone*:

> I been hangin' on threads
> I been playin' it straight
> Now, I've just got to cut loose
> Before it gets late . . .

The well-named *Dirge* shows the degree to which, on this record, Dylan has already returned to his old ways of viewing the relationships between people. It is a looking-back-at-love song with a vengeance, cold and detached, casting a jaundiced eye back over an affair that appears at first glance to be long dead and gone. "I hate myself for loving you / And the weakness that it showed", the song opens; the lover is seen as "just a painted face / On a trip down Suicide Road" and he says that he's "glad the curtain fell". The plain speaking recalls some of the 1965–66 songs:

> Can't recall a useful thing
> You ever did for me

> 'Cept pat me on the back one time
> When I was on my knees

but some subtler effects are also in evidence. Once he leaves an idea hanging in mid-air: "And the mercy that you showed to me / Whoever would have guessed" – the scene shifts and we never learn what there was to be guessed. The richest ambiguity however occurs in the closing lines:

> I hate myself for lovin' you
> But I should get over that

Does he mean that he should get over loving her, or get over hating himself for loving her? And does "should" mean "ought to" or "probably will"? The lines can be read in four possible ways. We notice too a change that has taken place in the course of the song: at the beginning the love was thought of as being in the past – "the weakness that it *showed*" – but by the end it is being spoken of as something with which he is still, apparently, burdened. It is a very troubled Dylan who sings this song, one who has little in common with the man who a moment later will sing 'You Angel You'. The Dylan of 'Dirge' is someone "Searching for a gem" in an "age of fiberglass", and who has "paid the price of solitude" for so doing. It is difficult to square this with the protestations of undying, untroubled love which had been his stock-in-trade for so long. Perhaps that is what he is thinking of, rather than something outside himself, when he sings

> The naked truth is still tabu
> Whenever it can be seen.

'Something There Is About You' is another song of restlessness, and seems to be about Dylan's effort to get back to a true view of himself and his aims. It is addressed to someone who evokes something, "I can't quite put my finger on", but which is associated with his roots and the values which they symbolise. There is a livingness and fluidity about the music that endows the words with a sense more poignant than nostalgic:

> Thought I'd shaken the wonder
> And the phantoms of my youth.
> Rainy days on the Great Lakes
> Walkin' the hills of old Duluth.
> There was me and Danny Lopez
> Cold eyes, black night and then there was Ruth.
> Somethin' there is about you
> That brings back a long-forgotten truth.

HOW DOES IT FEEL?

It is a sense of the validity of this felt but undefined truth, and of commitment to it, which determines the seriousness of his attitude towards the lover who is "the soul of many things".

> I could say that I'd be faithful
> I could say it in one sweet easy breath.
> But to you that would be cruelty
> And to me it surely would be death.

This is in effect a repudiation of his most cherished stances of the previous six years, which he had devoted mainly to saying just such things "in one sweet easy breath" – a phrase which, as Dylan sings it, beautifully gives form to the idea it expresses. He now clearly announces his intention to opt for full creative life instead of the easy half-life which he has been singing about since giving up the inner struggle undertaken in *John Wesley Harding* – something which will be discussed in a later chapter.

4

In *Blood on the Tracks* Dylan faces up to the failure of his vision of ideal love, and the integrity with which he does so brings its artistic rewards. Musically, there is a wider variety of mood and greater emotional range than on any album since *Blonde on Blonde,* and "that amazing urgency of communication – that arresting quality, that abrasive 'presence'", the loss of which on the subsequent L.P.'s Michael Gray has lamented,[11] is very much back with us: all the tracks are bloodstained. Most of them deal in one way or another with the feelings which arise from broken relationships, though there is one light-hearted song of flighty love, 'You're Gonna Make Me Lonesome When You Go', and 'Buckets of Rain', while it is a sad song underneath, partly shares in that mood. Some of the songs I shall discuss in the next chapter, which is devoted to Dylan's narrative technique, while the superb 'If You See Her, Say Hello' has already been mentioned in connection with the early love songs.

'Idiot Wind' is Dylan's most ambitious song since 'Visions of Johanna'. It is, I think, one of those works which make their fullest impact fairly early in one's acquaintance with them, whereas others – on this particular album I am thinking especially of 'Simple Twist of Fate' and 'Tangled Up in Blue' – are slower to reveal their riches, and consequently grow more. I thought 'Idiot Wind' a masterpiece when I first heard it, and still find it a great song, but I am more aware now of qualifications that need to be made. It is a kind of 'Desolation Row' of the spirit: whereas the earlier song deals with the interaction of society and self, the stress in 'Idiot Wind' is more on the personal. Its tone is a new one: sour, abrasive and disillusioned, yet almost ecstatically so, almost celebratory, as in the lines "I've been double-crossed now / For the very last time and now I'm finally FREE", where Dylan nearly howls the last word. The title phrase is mouthed in a way that seems to give physical form to the idea – "You're an idiot, babe, / It's a wonder that you still know how to breathe." The strength of the initial impact comes from the sheer enormity of Dylan's passion: the quality of wholesale vindictiveness has no parallel except in 'Positively 4th Street':

> You hurt the ones that I love best
> And cover up the truth with lies
> One day you'll be in the ditch
> Flies buzzin' around your eyes
> Blood on your saddle . . .

The attitude is however much more complex than in the earlier hate song; for one thing Dylan acknowledges a certain sense of shame which seems to be aroused as much by his own feelings as by his situation vis-à-vis the woman he is lambasting, a sense registered for instance by the image of his crawling past her door. Nor is he presenting a simplistic, black-and-white picture of the relationship:

> You'll never know the hurt I suffered
> Nor the pain I rise above
> And I'll never know the same about you
> Your holiness or your kind of love
> And it makes me feel
> So sorry . . .

This passage, though, localises the main weakness of the song. Dylan is uneasily aware here of something in himself which he "placed", with perfect artistic aplomb, in 'Visions of Johanna'. For in the embarrassing first two lines just quoted he "brags of his misery", exactly like the little boy lost in that song. The parade of emotion is too close to self-parody for comfort, and the statement is uncharacteristically generalised. Moreover the self-dramatisation is not sufficiently confident to be carried off: he is too conscious of the need to be fair (something that never crossed his mind in 'Positively 4th Street', and achieves in the lines that follow an objective balance that is very uneasy and strikes us as a bit mechanistic, as if it were done out of duty rather than real feeling. Indeed the last two lines, coming in a song which has reached such heights (or depths) of vindictive intensity, are in danger of sounding insincere. I don't think they quite do so; but we remain uncomfortably aware of the danger that he has avoided by the skin of his teeth. This hump over, Dylan *is* able, in the final lines of the song, to take upon himself an equal share of the blame in a way that does not suggest hypocrisy:

> Idiot wind
> Blowing through the dust upon our shelves
> We're idiots, babe
> It's a wonder we can even feed ourselves.

The change from the familiar condemnatory refrain of the previous verses is effective and moving; but it has been a close-run thing. The result is less perfectly achieved than with the similar device at the end of 'One Too Many Mornings'; but then 'Idiot Wind' is a very much more complicated and ambitious song.

As in 'Visions of Johanna', the "I" character is projected through various personas. In the first verse he is depicted, in a way that no doubt has autobiographical connotations, as a victim of press rumour, accused of shooting "a man named Gray" and taking his wife to Italy – this is the occasion for a characteristic shaft of black wit:

> She inherited a million bucks
> And when she died it came to me
> I can't help it if I'm lucky . . .

The self-dramatisation extends in verse two to the association of his sufferings with those of Christ on the cross; while in the third a fresh persona is momentarily adopted in what I have been told (though I can't confirm it) is a reference to the film *Bonnie and Clyde*:

> I waited for you on the running boards
> Near the cypress tree while the springtime turned
> Slowly into autumn.

The shifting, fragmented imagery is however held together by the consistency of the feeling and the uncompromising extremity of its expression, so that the song operates in a way which makes its flaws less important in practice than they look on paper.

'Shelter from the Storm' has no great profundity of meaning but has shown itself to be a strong and versatile song which adapts well to different moods and musical interpretations. The original version, for instance, is light, detached and almost casual in approach, the *Hard Rain* one full-blooded and emotional, that on the *Budokan* L.P. tight, sombre and intense, though the backing is rich and nostalgic. Dylan looks back with regret at the breakdown of a relationship which once afforded him solace and protection, and he is ready here to accept the blame: "I took too much for granted / Got my signals crossed" (lines which he delivers, particularly on *Blood on the Tracks*, with a rather throwaway air, as if to say, "Well, that's just the way it was."). Much of the song's strength lies in the cumulative effects of its imagery in imparting depth to the basically simple story:

> I was burned out from exhaustion
> Buried in the hail
> Poisoned in the bushes
> An' blown out on the trail.
> Hunted like a crocodile
> Ravaged in the corn...

In contemplating the end of the bond of which he sings Dylan is torn between optimism and pessimism, between regressive longing and the impulse to put the past behind him and strike out into the future. He does not attempt an artificial resolution of this conflict but allows the song to maintain the balance of forces between the opposites, and thus reflect the reality of his mixed and equivocal feelings:

> I've heard newborn babies wailin' like a mornin' dove
> And old men with broken teeth
> Stranded without love
> Do I understand your question, man
> Is it hopeless and forlorn
> "Come in," she said, "I'll give you
> Shelter from the storm."

The simple poignancy of the thought that the old men with broken teeth were once newborn babies with all of life ahead of them, and that all such babies may one day be similarly "stranded without love", derives largely from its not being explicitly stated; while in the latter part of the verse Dylan makes good use of a favourite device when he leaves the resulting question unanswered. A similar effect of leaving emotions unresolved is achieved in the last verse when the confident "Beauty walks the razor's edge / Some day I'll make it mine" is immediately followed by the backward-looking "If I could only turn back the clock / To when God and her were born". This underlying irresolution, this sense of being lost and uncertain where to go next, is the very feeling which the song aims at expressing.

The most important difference between the Dylan of *Blood on the Tracks* and that of the earlier love songs is the extent to which he is prepared to admit not only his own vulnerability (he did that in for instance 'Boots of Spanish Leather') but also his own blame. We have never before heard him plead, as he does in 'You're a Big Girl Now', 'I can change, I swear ...'

> Love is so simple

HOW DOES IT FEEL?

> To quote a phrase
> You've known it all the time
> I'm learnin' it these days . . .

The savage irony with which he enunciates that "to quote a phrase" recognises, perhaps, that his own obeisances to the cliché of simple love during his country period were ill-directed — he was losing hold of the reality even while pursuing its phantom. The expression of pain in this little song — and in 'Meet Me in the Morning', which is similar in mood and theme — is more effective than the parade of emotion in 'Idiot Wind' because it is quite undiluted by anger :

> I'm going out of my mind
> Oh – oh
> With a pain that stops and starts
> Like a corkscrew to my heart
> Ever since we've been apart.

In songs like these, and particularly in 'If You See Her, Say Hello', Dylan shows a new readiness to communicate his feelings very directly, in a style that is quite unadorned and often shorn of imagery. This new emotional openness obviates the need to adopt some of the subtle artistic stratagems which were required to maintain balance in many of the earlier songs where he was taking some strong defensive line. One result is that, precisely because of their clean-cut efficiency, there is often little in these recent love songs that calls for comment — the critic can do little more than point to them. Another consequence is that music and expression contribute more, proportionately, to total sense than in songs where the lyrics are more complex. This is obviously true of the two love songs on *Desire*, 'Oh Sister' and 'Sara'. The verbal message of the former is executed with swift economy, but the music elaborates the feeling in waves of passionate sound. There is more imagery in 'Sara', but it is of a simple evocative kind. It works, though, especially the contrasting, sharply realised pictures of the beach: first as seen by Dylan from the dunes in the opening verses, with the children playing with their pails and "the shells / fallin' out of their hands", and then, in the last verse, "deserted"

> Except for some kelp
> And a piece of an old ship
> That lies on the shore.

(Dylan has denied, incidentally, that the song is necessarily about his wife;[12] but I think we can take this as in effect an insistence on the autonomy of the work of art and of the irrelevance of autobiography as an element in its appreciation.)

VOICE WITHOUT RESTRAINT

From *Desire* onwards the excitement of Dylan's lyrics lies for the most part in areas other than the songs of personal relationship. It is as if, for the time being, he is allowing love to look after itself, perhaps feeling, as he did in "Buckets of Rain", that

> Life is sad, life is a bust
> All ya can do is do what you must
> You do what you must do
> And ya do it well . . .

All the same, there are some strong love songs on *Street-Legal*. 'New Pony' is a powerful, demonic piece, but like 'Lay Lady Lay' it is about desire rather than emotion: "Come over here, pony, I, / I wanna climb up one time on you." 'Is Your Love in Vain?' is unusual in anticipating love rather than looking back at it, with Dylan somewhat reluctantly resolving to "take a chance", at the same time contriving to cock a satirical snook at Women's Lib with the lines

> Can you cook and sew, make flowers grow?
> Do you understand my pain?

The tune is rich and anthem-like, and its ending sounds like a parody – possibly intentional – of that of 'Onward, Christian Soldiers'. The other songs in the group take the customary rear-view mirror view of love. The least successful is 'True Love Tends to Forget'; while lacking in structural complexity and memorable imagery it is also vague and ill-defined – for once no real sense is forthcoming of what feeling Dylan is trying to put over. Not so with 'We Better Talk This Over', in which every line says something solid and exact, the new style of economic directness working at its most efficient. The tone is realistic and unemotional but the valediction sympathetic and mature. This is not one of the open-ended songs: he takes care to shut the door quietly but firmly on "the bond that we've both gone beyond":

> It'd be great to cross paths in a day and a half
> Look at each other and laugh.
> But I don't think it's liable to happen,
> Like the sound of one hand clappin'.
> The vows that we kept are now broken and swept
> 'Neath the bed where we slept.

The last song on the record is an exception to the rule of simplicity and austere statement. 'Where Are You Tonight? (Journey Through Dark Heat)' is impressionistic, allusive, difficult, full of striking and colourful imagery. With 'Changing of the Guards', 'Señor', and to some extent 'No Time To Think', it belongs to a group of songs on *Street-Legal* which stand up as very impressive poetry when seen on the page, to a degree equalled in Dylan's earlier work perhaps only by 'Visions of Johanna'; and which look almost as if they might have been written as poems, which 'Johanna' doesn't. 'Where Are You Tonight?' is also one of Dylan's most powerful *songs*, with a musical pattern which works *with* the words – which is not entirely true of 'Changing of the Guards' (a point that will be examined in a later chapter). In general type it is similar to 'Visions of Johanna' and 'Idiot Wind', centring on the vicissitudes of a love relation but sending its shock waves far out beyond that centre; and like them its structure is a mosaic, building up a complex mood out of a series of separate impressions which often have little overt connection with each other, but which in some way fit together as part of a schematic whole. They do so, I suppose, because they all arise out of a single nucleus of feelings in Dylan himself; the images act as intermediaries between him and us, working on our senses until we begin to "feel" the situation as he feels it. More than feeling is communicated, though; while much remains obscure, enough factual information is thrown out here and there to provide us with a frame onto which, like plants, the feelings can attach themselves, and thus assume body, form and shape.

The pieces of the mosaic are formed by four-line units of meaning which also correspond to musical units. This pattern is adhered to pretty consistently throughout the song, with, at the most, tenuous observable connections between the consecutive elements, and more often none. This can be illustrated by the opening of the song, which illuminates the sub-title, "Journey Through Dark Heat". The song is conceived as a journey from despair to hope:

> There's a long-distance train rolling through the rain,
> Tears on the letter I write.
> There's a woman I long to touch, and I miss her so much,
> But she's drifting like a satellite.

The railroad imagery is of course one of Dylan's staple recourses but it never seems to lose its fascination for him or its serviceableness in his hands. His talent for building up a vivid picture with a few strokes is characteristically effective here: we can see the rain on the train window and perhaps the tears – which, thanks to the solid external context in which they are set, don't seem histrionic this time – making the ink run on the paper; then Dylan (or whoever it is) looking out at the darkening landscape, watching the moon drifting through the clouds, and visualising the woman he misses as just such a drifting satellite. We wonder, too, whether we are also to read its metaphorical meaning into the word "satellite": is the woman now the satellite of some other man? With the next lines

there is a swift change of scene; the unit that follows is this time sub-
divided, its two sets of images together building up the sense of that
"dark heat" through which the singer journeys.

> There's a neon light ablaze in this green smoky haze,
> Laughter down on Elizabeth Street,
> And a lonesome bell tone in that valley of stone
> Where she bathed in a stream of pure heat.

The first two lines evoke vividly a hot, claustrophobic, typically
urban scene which stands in potent contrast to the melancholy
austerity of the train journey, and introduces through a physical
image a suggestion of confusion and fogginess which has to do with
the *emotional* background of the story. That laughter, while it may
not necessarily be hostile, strikes us as having an excluding, almost
mocking ring to it: Dylan (and with him ourselves) is looking in on
a scene to which he is not admitted. The final lines contribute a
further element to the total ground of feeling which Dylan wants to
spread out and build upon: the sense of sterile passion. The chosen
image, though not realistic, is again strongly visualised: the naked
woman is there before our eyes, bathing in the steaming water of
that valley of unyielding stone. The "lonesome bell tone" which
sounds in the distance associates this passion with a feeling of
sadness and doom.

Throughout the song an almost cinematic clarity is maintained:
though the little scenes are often surreal the imagery points towards
meaning, it does not appear to be exhibiting itself for its own sake as
did, on occasions, the imagery of the *Bringing It all Back Home /
Blonde on Blonde* era. The "babe in the arms of a woman in a rage";
the sight of someone climbing up a girl's hair to discover "her invis-
ible self": the "foot in the face" of "the guy you were lovin'"; the
"juice running down my leg" after Dylan has bitten "into the root
of forbidden fruit"; "the white diamond gloom on the dark side of
this room": all, as well as presenting us with sharply realised pictures, move the story forward, inform us and help us to "realise"
what the song is about, not so much in our minds as through our
senses. There is also the more specific information that serves as the
song's frame. We learn that the couple have parted and that "I" has
left town; the "long-time golden-haired stripper" who appears on
the stage and "winds back the clock, and . . turns back the page / Of
a book that nobody can write" suggests a triangular situation; but
the figure becomes quadrilateral with the arrival on the scene of the
"guy you were lovin'"; there has been conflict, acrimony and ill-
feeling. As we have become used to expecting in this type of song,
identities are not always clearly defined. The main female character
is sometimes "she" and sometimes "you". It is not apparent

46

whether "Her father" is the same as the "full-blooded Cherokee" of verse two, or whether the "He" who "took good center-aim but ... missed just the same" is to be confounded with "the guy you were lovin'". "Marcel and St John", those 'strong men belittled by doubt" with whom Dylan leaves town, are also uncertain quantities, though probably they are fragments of his own personality. These characteristic unclarities are part of Dylan's design on us: he is setting out not to make us understand but to make us feel, and we are more likely to feel when our minds are not in control, when the "meddling intellect", as Wordsworth called it, has not pre-empted our responses.

The feeling, of course, comes also from the music. There is a largeness about it, almost an exaltation, a sense of heights and depths, which matches the lyrics and Dylan's whole-spirited delivery. The theme of spiritual struggle in the song – "I fought with my twin, that enemy within, / Till both of us fell by the way" – is enacted, not merely declaimed, so that we sense that the promise that is held out at the end by that "pathway that leads up to the stars" is not a conventional postulate but something that has indeed been paid for with Dylan's scars. Moreover the phrase "sweet paradise" is not, I think, meant to be taken quite straight. The words are coloured with an irony whose force is brought out by the final words of the song:

There's a new day at dawn, and I've finally arrived,
If I'm there in the morning, baby, you'll know I've survived.
I can't believe it; I can't believe I'm alive.
But without you, it just doesn't seem right.
Oh, where are you tonight?

With *Slow Train Coming* Dylan embarks on a very different kind of relationship from those he tells about in the songs we have been looking at in this chapter (though it may have a lot more in common with them than we might imagine). There is however one place in 'Precious Angel' in which human love bubbles happily to the surface, with an image which makes us think of that ambivalent hymn of 1965, 'She Belongs To Me', with its eloquent lines, "She can take the dark out of the nighttime / And paint the daytime black." The contrast in mood with what follows needs no underlining:

You're the queen of my flesh, girl; you're my woman,
    you're my delight.
You're the lamp of my soul, girl, and you torch up the night.

The joyful straightforwardness to which Dylan has come in this – so different, too, from the anodyne "love" of the country songs – makes a good note on which to end this part of the study.

Chapter Three

Telling The Story

"The simplest way I can tell the story." All Dylan's songs tell a story, in a general sense; and indeed storytelling lies at the root of all literary art, whether oral or written. Yet until comparatively recently storytelling songs in the more restricted sense – those which have a basis of continuous narrative – have not been prominent in his output. His imagination is notably non-linear; as we have seen, he prefers to build up a mood or feeling through a patchwork of discrete impressions, although these may be linked together in more or less subtle ways by a variety of devices and associations. His units of meaning have tended, typically, to be many and local. When he does use narrative on the albums prior to *Blood on the Tracks* it tends to be in ways which undermine the principles of normal logical progression: on the one hand he mocks those principles in songs which recreate with remarkable grasp the fantastic movements of dreams with their distorted, subliminal kinds of logic and their swift metamorphoses and transitions ('Motorpsycho Nightmare', 'Bob Dylan's 115th Dream'); and on the other he parodies the reproduction of an undifferentiated "slice of life" in a song like the marvellously deadpan 'Clothes Line'.

The seeming antagonism to linear progression is probably in part temperamental, in part a natural consequence of the artistic conditions under which Dylan creates his songs, conditions which call for immediacy of impact rather than the slow savouring of experience. It is also possible that the drug experience may have modified his habits of perception at a crucial stage in his artistic development. It is true that there are a number of early protest songs which have a simple narrative structure, but in most of these the point lies in the moral rather than in the telling of a tale for its own sake. The finest of them is 'The Ballad of Hollis Brown', in which the moral is less explicit, contained by the events rather than extracted from them, the view of life darker and more ambiguous than that of, say, 'The Lonesome Death of Hattie Carroll':

> There's seven people dead
> On a South Dakota farm

48

TELLING THE STORY

Somewhere in the distance
There's seven new people born

It is relevant to the concerns of this chapter that this very effective song is conceived as a traditional ballad.

Given this background it is at first sight odd that, on *Blood on the Tracks* and *Desire*, narrative songs not only acquire unwonted prominence but provide one of the most exciting departures in Dylan's art for many years. Two influences are easily recognisable here – those of the cinema and of the ballad. Dylan has apparently always been interested in the cinema, but in a more active way since his involvement in *Pat Garrett and Billy the Kid*. It is unlikely to be coincidence that these songs, with their very marked visual qualities and their method of telling a story by presenting a series of differentiated and individually conceived scenes in progressive sequence but without connective devices, were being written during the period that led up to Dylan's filming of *Renaldo and Clara*; the correspondence of this procedure to cinematic montage techniques is clear. It has even more marked affinities, though, with the characteristic features of the ballads of the oral tradition. I think it is likely that the impetus to try writing narrative songs came from Dylan's interest in the cinema, in that this suggested to him ways in which he could tell stories without doing violence to his established and preferred artistic habits; and that when he came to put this impulse into practice he found himself making extensive use of techniques and formulae which he had absorbed from contact with the oral tradition in his "folk-singing" days, and – more importantly – sharing in similar tendencies of mind.

It is generally assumed that Dylan's involvement in the "purist" folk revival was a fleeting and somewhat superficial matter which left little permanent trace on his mature work, and was perhaps even dictated, at least in part, by self-interest – as the road to fame most open to him at the time he was pursuing it. This is a view which various remarks made by Dylan himself have done something to encourage, but I think that it is an oversimplified one. It is one of the underlying themes of the present study that Dylan carries over into radically changed cultural conditions many of the values and distinguishing features of oral and verbal folk tradition. (I don't of course mean by that just the traditions of balladry and oral minstrelsy which crossed the Atlantic and took root in American soil, but the indigenous growths such as the blues, gospel music and the various "poor white" musical traditions – which *overall* are more important contributors to his total artistic heritage.) That such tradition should remain active and developing in the age of electronic communication is not in itself at all surprising; nor does it in the least depend on Dylan, or any individual, in that respect. What *is* important and indicative is that it can be identified as a living force in the work of one who is not, in any but a totally new sense, a folk artist, but a literate, and indeed lettered, inheritor of a totally different Western tradition: that of the individual artist giving expression to an individual vision peculiar to himself, his way of "seeing" the world. Throughout the history of post-medieval Western culture these strands of popular and "high" art (the split originates in that between oral and literate art, but since the advent of general literacy can no longer be defined in those terms) have remained quite separate and indeed grown farther apart. In Dylan they come together for the first time in one who is, in the terms of the "élite" tradition, a major artist; and they do so because of the rise of an aural (though not *oral*) culture which is still however verbal. Dylan communicates an individual vision which is in one of its dimensions verbal, but he communicates it through the ear and not through the eye. It is natural that in so doing he should fall heir to some of the traditions of those who communicated a communal vision through the ear because the eye was closed to the word, for them and their audience – the "illiterate" creators of oral literature and its music.

In order to develop this heritage creatively as an element in his own art – and to gain the freedom, of course, to do many other things too – it was necessary for Dylan to turn away from the pseudo-purist pieties of the folk-revival. The oft-quoted disparaging memark about Joan Baez "still singing about Mary Hamilton"[1] does not imply a rejection of the artistic values contained in folk song, but a rejection of certain restrictive attitudes towards those values. As I hope to show, the influence of the ballads on Dylan's work goes much deeper than is usually recognised; and not only in the fairly recent narrative songs which will be the main subject of this chapter. In his immediate "folk" period there are some obvious modellings of songs or motifs on balladic originals, notably the borrowing of the question-and-answer structure of 'Lord Randal' for 'It's a Hard Rain's A-Gonna Fall':

> O where hae ye been, Lord Randal, my son?
> O where hae ye been, my handsome young man?

> Oh, where have you been, my blue-eyed son?
> Oh, where have you been, my darling young one?

More fundamental however than this well-known instance is Dylan's habit of switching persons in the course of a song – usually from referring to someone in the third person to addressing them in the second, or vice versa. We have already in the previous chapter noticed the workings of this device in 'One Too Many Mornings' and 'Don't Think Twice, It's All Right'. Similar effects of dramatic heightening are frequently encountered in the ballads, though the change here is more often between the *first* and third persons. The opening verse of most versions of 'The Banks of Red Roses', for instance, is a first person narrative, while the last recounts, in the third person, the murder of the erstwhile narrator. The transition (in italics) occurs thus in the middle verse:

> On the banks o' red roses my love and I sat down,
> He took out his tuning-box to play *his love* a tune.
> In the middle o' the tune, his love broke down and cried,
> "Oh my Johnnie, oh my Johnnie dinna leave me."

The effect is aided by the line of direct speech, which serves to distract our attention from the transition so that it is rendered unobtrusive until the process is made complete by the dramatic action of the last stanza. In 'Barbara Allan' (which, for the record, makes an appearance in *Tarantula*), a similar device occurs: the transition from first to third person is "concealed" by an entire stanza of direct speech between the protagonists. This may be compared with what happens in 'Just Like a Woman'. We are aware, when Dylan sings "Ah, you fake just like a woman" in the last chorus, that there has been a transition from its previous form: "She takes just like a woman" etc. This does not seem to have happened abruptly, but until we know the song well we are probably not quite sure how it has been achieved. The answer lies in the connecting passage which links the second and final verses and prepares for the switch:

> It was raining from the first
> And I was dying of thirst
> So I came in here
> And *your* long-time curse hurts
> But what's worse
> Is this pain in here
> I can't stay in here
> Ain't it clear that –
>
> I just can't fit
> Yes, I believe it's time for us to quit . . .

There is another important feature of ballad composition variants of which we find in Dylan's writing: the communication of a crucial event in a narrative by implication rather than direct statement. This habit accords well with the stanza-by-stanza structure which so many of Dylan's songs share with the ballad tradition, but it becomes particularly evident and effective in his narrative songs. Perhaps the most famous example in Scottish balladry is the way we learn of the deaths of the three sons in 'The Wife of Usher's Well':

> It fell about the Martinmas
>   When nights are lang and mirk
> The carline wife's three sons came hame,
>   And their hats were o' the birk.
>
> It neither grew in syke nor ditch,
>   Nor yet in ony sheugh;
> But at the gates o' Paradise
>   That birk grew fair eneugh.

A less moving and dramatic instance, but one which we can definitely link with Dylan, occurs in 'The Bonnie Lass o' I yvie'. He recorded an Americanised and highly telescoped but still recognisable version of this song on his first album, under the title 'Pretty Peggy-O'. (The track is worth listening to, if only to savour the way Dylan deals with the phrase "died for a maid".) The implication in question is that of the refusal of the Captain's plea that the troop should remain until the completion of his wooing:

> But the Colonel he cries "Now mount, boys, mount!"
> The captain he cries "Oh tarry-o.
> Oh gang nae awa' for anither day or twa
> Till we see if this bonnie lass will marry-o."
>
> It was early next morning that we rode awa'
> And oh but our captain was sorry-o.
> The drums they did beat owre the bonnie braes o' Gight
> An' the band played The Lowlands o' Fyvie-o.

Dylan's narrative songs will be seen to yield many examples of this type of procedure. It matters little whether these likenesses are the result of direct influence, either conscious or unconscious, or whether they arise more from a certain community of circumstance between Dylan and the ballad composers which caused both to approach the making of their songs in analogous ways. In either case they indicate a similarity of temper, of cast of mind, and stance towards the world and their material, which makes it justifiable to suggest that in some measure Dylan's work perpetuates ballad traditions in a living way.

Before turning to the narrative songs of *Blood on the Tracks* and *Desire* I want to look briefly at some features of a few earlier songs which prefigure them. All are comic in spirit and vision, which separates them sharply from the later stories, but they also have a number of revealing features in common with them. The most obvious is their sharply visualised quality. 'Motorpsycho Nightmare' is a kind of comic rider to Alfred Hitchcock's *Psycho*, describing the experience (whether it's a sleeping or waking nightmare is not made clear) of someone whose imagination has been over-extended by seeing the famous thriller, so it is not surprising that it has a strong cinematic flavour. Its narrative is however more con-nected than that of 'Bob Dylan's 115th Dream', the stanzas not being conceived and realised as separate entities to the same degree: the sequence is more or less logical though the events themselves are crazy enough. It is a very funny piece of preposterous storytelling, but Dylan doesn't know how to finish it. The story really ends with the narrator running off, down the road away from the nightmare farmhouse as the sun comes up, and the enraged farmer preparing to fire at him; and Dylan could very satisfactorily have left us with that picture. But he feels the need to round off the song and to sum it up, and he adds a most unsatisfactory coda which only minimally extends the joke and finished with four lines intended as a kind of light-hearted *moralitas*, which fall exceedingly flat:

> Me, I romp and stomp,
> Thankful as I romp,
> Without freedom of speech,
> I might be in the swamp.

Many ballads, too, end with a kind of coda. Dylan shows, in his subsequent narratives, a great fondness for this device, and the above early attempt is cited only for reasons of contrast with the variety and complexity of his several later, successful essays in a similar exercise.

The problem of how to end his song is solved in 'Bob Dylan's 115th Dream' in a different way, which again has numerous balladic precedents: he "frames" the action between corresponding opening and closing stanzas. The first verse has the ship sailing towards the American coast:

> I was riding in the Mayflower
> When I thought I spied some land
> I yelled for Captain Arab . . .

Thus, within the space of the first three lines, the three epic Ameri-can voyages are conflated: those of Columbus, the Pilgrim Fathers, and the *'Pequod'*. (Ballads – yet again – tend to arrange their material in groupings of three. That Columbus is included in the trip by means of the phrase "I thought I spied some land" is made clear by the second verse: "'I think I'll call it America'/I said as we hit land.") The subject of the song is, in fact, the comic "discovery" of contemporary America by the narrator. When this hilarious jaunt is complete he makes it "back to the ship", and the last verse has him sailing out as the first had him sailing in:

VOICE WITHOUT RESTRAINT

> When I was leavin' the bay
> I saw three ships a-sailin'
> They were all heading my way
> I asked the captain what his name was
> And how come he didn't drive a truck
> He said his name was Columbus
> I just said "Good luck."

The circular pattern of the song is neatly completed by his meeting with the three ships of Columbus' fleet. The ironic wit of the punch-line is characteristic. As the man about to discover the America whose future the song has just presented to us, Columbus could be said to need all the luck he can get.

'Clothes Line Saga' faithfully retails a sequence of doings of absolutely no significance by which a single event of great public and private moment is overwhelmed and smothered out of existence. Clothes are brought in from the line, found to be wet, and taken back out again: the night passes, the clothes are felt, and finally they are brought in once more. In the midst of these absorbing pursuits a passing neighbour casually imparts a piece of news:

> "Have you heard the news?" he said with a grin,
> "The Vice-President's gone mad!"
> "Where?" "Downtown." "When?" "Last night."
> "Hmmm, say, that's too bad!"
> "Well, there's nothin' we can do about it," said the neighbour,
> "It's just somethin' we're gonna have to forget."
> "Yes, I guess so," said Mama,
> Then she asked me if the clothes were still wet.

One shouldn't really discuss such a song: the very act of talking about it gives an impression of a solemnity which is quite at odds with its spirit. All the same, I dare to call attention to something which is relevant to Dylan's future narrative methods. In 'Clothes Line Saga' he says much, in a comic way, about human nature without seeming to be saying anything at all. A set of events is recorded in a completely flat and impartial manner; some people make some flat and commonplace remarks; that is all. No comment, no imagery, no action worthy of the name; only a set of responses that are very recognisable and quite inappropriate. By the adroit selection and disposing of the most unpromising and insubstantial material Dylan has said something about the way things are, the way people are, and has made us laugh about it; it has all been done by the simplest – or the most apparently simple – of narrative means.

TELLING THE STORY

2

Blood on the Tracks kicks off with two songs with a new storytelling form – 'Tangled Up in Blue' and 'Simple Twist of Fate' – and side two includes another, the epic 'Lily, Rosemary and the Jack of Hearts'. Of these the last-named probably makes the greatest initial impression; the other two are more subtle, deceptive songs, susceptible – particularly 'Tangled Up in Blue' – to widely differing interpretations. It is only recently that I have reached the conclusion that since its release I have been listening to 'Tangled Up in Blue' and understanding it quite wrongly. I had assumed (without looking closely at the text) that the song describes a single obsessive relationship, that of a couple who, through a series of admittedly unlikely coincidences, keep crossing paths, joining up and splitting again, and that the final verse looks forward to a further instalment in this saga. I am now convinced that this was entirely wrong: only the "she"'s of the first and last verses are the same, the intervening stanzas describing the narrator's various affairs with other women as he moves restlessly about the country with the memory of his first love still remaining stubbornly at the back of his mind. That may seem a grotesque mistake for me to have made, but it seems that I shared it with many others.[2] I suspect that Dylan intends us to make it and then, perhaps, realise that we were wrong: he enjoys manipulating his audience in such ways. (As I shall indicate in the next chapter, I believe almost the *whole* of *John Wesley Harding* to have such an intention – and that in that case the deception has been all too successful.) There are certainly a number of carefully placed phrases in 'Tangled Up in Blue' that might encourage us to jump to the wrong conclusion – if we are listening with insufficient alertness of attention – but which do not in fact carry the implications we take them to have at all. Of course, not everybody may be deceived.

I spoke of the balladic "framing" device which forms the basic structure of 'Bob Dylan's 115th Dream': 'Tangled Up in Blue' is similarly constructed. The song begins:

> Early one mornin' the sun was shinin'
> I was layin' in bed
> Won'drin' if she'd changed at all
> If her hair was still red.

The narrator goes on to tell what split the couple up, presumably a long time ago, namely the opposition of "her folks": "They never did like Mama's home-made dress / Papa's bank book wasn't big enough." (Familial opposition is a typical obstacle to true love in the ballads.) The song's first ambiguity follows:

VOICE WITHOUT RESTRAINT

And I was standin' on the side of the road
Rain fallin' on my shoes
Headin' out for the east coast . . .

Does this refer to the start of the travels which the song recounts,
after he has parted from the girl? I used to think so, but now I think
that it is the song's *final* journey, to which he has been driven by those
memories that he had as he "was layin' in bed". It is the last verse,
not the second, with which it connects:

So now I'm goin' back again
I got to get to her somehow . . .

Dylan's deception, if we may call it that, is based fundamentally
on something very simple: the use of the word "she" to refer to all
the women he tells us of, without any differentiating description.
No matter how well we know Dylan, our linear, print-orientated
prejudices lead us to expect continuity from one stanza to the next.
Thus when the second verse begins, "She was married when we
first met / Soon to be divorced", we tend to assume that he is still
talking about the same woman, even though something seems
wrong – a woman about to be divorced would not be likely to
worry about the attitudes of her "folks" when choosing a new mate.
But see how Dylan encourages our false expectations. He describes
how this couple split up:

She turned around to look at me
As I was walkin' away
I heard her say over her shoulder
"We'll meet again some day
On the avenue"

Still with the vague idea in our heads that the girls of the first and
second verses are the same, we are now encouraged to expect the
couple to meet up once more. The process of setting up a false assumption in our minds about the whole theme and movement of the
song has been initiated. In the third stanza the hero is on his own: he
has a job working as a cook in "the great north woods" until the axe
falls one day ("But I never did like it all that much" sings Dylan
with assumed casualness, in one of his marvellous flashes of psychological observation – it is what everyone says when the axe has
fallen, and the way they say it too); then he drifts south. But the *first*
woman (as I now believe it to be) is still in his thoughts:

But all the while I was alone
The past was close behind

TELLING THE STORY

> I seen a lot of women
> But she never escaped my mind . . .

Our assumption about the composite couple of our imagination being about to run up against each other again is thus reinforced. So we come to verse four:

> She was workin' in a topless place
> And I stopped in for a beer
> I just kept lookin' at the side of her face
> In the spotlight so clear . . .

Of course he is looking at the side of her face just because he is attracted to her; but we imagine it is because he thinks he recognises her. We may begin to feel that we were wrong when he prepares to leave, but then the girl asks, "Don't I know your name?" Again we are deceived: we think of it as the long-awaited lovers' reunion, when in fact the remark is no more than a standard opening gambit. In the same way, when we hear the words "She studied the lines on my face", we think of the woman observing the ageing process and musing on how he has changed, whereas really she is doing no more than studying the lines on his face. Our mistaken assumption (if we have once succumbed to it) is now so well established that everything seems to accord with it: verse five seems to be a continuation of verse four, and six to follow on from five. Actually the fifth verse depicts a further isolated scene which might or might not follow from its predecessors – there are no special pointers which can decide the matter one way or the other. "I thought you'd never say hello," this girl says as she offers the narrator a pipe and hands him a book of poems by a thirteenth-century Italian poet:

> And every one of them words rang true
> And glowed like burnin' coal
> Pourin' off of every page
> Like it was written in my soul
> From me to you
> Tangled up in blue

On my present understanding of the song, this vividly realised experience directs the narrator's feelings back once more towards his original love, the girl of the first stanza. That is the point of the sudden dramatic addressing of someone – "from me to you" – which occurs only at this point in the story. For all his experiences with other women serve only to remind him of the first; so that when, in verse six, yet another relationship goes sour and the only response he knows is "to keep on keepin' on / Like a bird that flew", he is ready to complete the circle by making his way back to the girl he left behind him at the beginning of his travelling.

I do not want to give the impression that the purpose of *Tangled Up in Blue* is merely to provide Dylan with an exercise in deception. I think merely that, from the composer's point of view, that element was something which provided interest and entertainment during the structuring of the song; and it happens to be structure with which this chapter is mainly concerned – how Dylan tells a story. The substance of the song, on the other hand, is principally atmospheric, the building up of scenes which vividly evoke times and places.

There is one further point which may be of some interest. In the final stanza, as the narrator prepares to go back to his first love after a long absence, he thinks back:

> All the people we used to know
> They're an illusion to me now
> Some are mathematicians
> Some are carpenters' wives . . .

The specificity of that contrast always seemed very striking to me; until I was browsing through the *Oxford Book of Ballads* and I noticed something in the ballad called *The Daemon Lover* which appeared to shed further light on it. This ballad takes up the familiar theme of the lover who returns after seven years (and *Tangled Up in Blue* has seven stanzas, which could correspond to seven years):

> 'O where hae ye been my long, long love,
>   These seven long years and more?'
> 'O I'm come to seek my former vows,
>   That ye promised me before.'

But she has bad news for him – she has "become a wife":

> 'I am married to a ship-carpenter,
>   A ship-carpenter he's bound, . . .'

The correspondence of both situation and phraseology may be no more than coincidence; but coincidence or not, it provides for me a further moving and ironical resonance to 'Tangled Up in Blue' by suggesting what might well await the returning lover when (and if) he does finally make it back home.

'Simple Twist of Fate' is an outstanding example of how Dylan can make a feeling real by embodying it in a simple but evocative narrative. "Here's a simple love story – happened to me," he says when he introduces the number on his *Budokan* record. That is not likely to imply that the events Dylan describes actually happened to him just that way: the song is presumably an "objective correlative", to borrow T. S. Eliot's phrase, for a much more ramified and extended complex of experience, reducing this complex to its essence and then making it concrete. The feeling it embodies is that of a great lost opportunity, nostalgically longed for, an opportunity at once gained and lost through "a simple twist of fate". This song is one of those to which Dylan looks (or looked) set to keep returning, and also one which seems to have a particularly unfixed and fluid character for him. The *Budokan* version shows numerous changes from the original, some of them minor, but including almost completely new fourth and final verses. Joan Baez has also recorded a version of it, with changes of her own, on *Diamonds and Rust*, taking off Dylan's voice in one verse for good measure. This quality of adaptability in 'Simple Twist of Fate' reflects its broadly impressionistic approach to telling the story.

The stage props of the tale have a mythic rather than a realistic character, they are almost the staple clichés of the fleeting love affair: the park at twilight, the walk by the canal, the beat-up hotel room (though the hotel has become "renovated" by the time Dylan reaches Budokan), the distant saxophone as the lady leaves him asleep, the note she leaves behind in the later version, the "waterfront docks" which suggest that she is the archetypal whore who turns out to have feelings. There is an element of consciously controlled cliché in some of the little scenes that are brought sharply before our vision:

> A saxophone someplace far off played
> As she was walkin' by the arcade
> As the light burst through a beat-up shade
> Where he was wakin' up
> She dropped a coin into the cup
> Of a blind man at the gate
> And forgot about a simple twist of fate.

Within this familiar but economically evoked setting the characters' confused feelings are briefly but convincingly sketched. One of Dylan's characteristic little touches of drama of which we have spoken before – "he" becoming "I" – is achieved with particular deftness in the lines:

> They walked along by the old canal
> A little confused I remember well
> And stopped into a strange hotel . . .

The poignancy of that is once more reminiscent of the ballads; in the romance of 'Thomas of Ersseldoune", which lies behind "True Thomas", we have this:

> Thomas dwelled in that solace,

VOICE WITHOUT RESTRAINT

> More than I you say, perdie;
> Till on a day, so have I grace,
> My lufely lady said to me: . . .

Part of the song's fluidity in Dylan's various treatments consists in the opportunity to transfer the feelings of one character to the other – the *Budokan* song makes the woman the main experiencing agent in the early verses, attributing to her the emotions which originally belong to the man. Some of the ways open to him of giving extra depth to his songs arise from his knowing that we can respond to new treatments out of the experience brought from previous ones – he can play on our expectations. Thus he makes a point here about the relativity of subjective experience which connects with the "You're right from your side / And I'm right from mine" of 'One Too Many Mornings', and the "I'll come and be crying to you" of 'To Ramona'. I felt it this way, he seems to be saying, but who knows?, maybe she was feeling it just the same way. Another interesting point relates to the use of tense. The first four verses use the preterite, but in verse five (the penultimate verse) Dylan adopts the historic present: "He hears the ticking of the clocks . . ." This serves to emphasise not only the immediacy of the story but its continuity with the narrator's *present* experience, its continuing reality to him; and so prepares for the reflective coda of the final verse: "People tell me it's a sin . . ."

The changes between the two officially recorded versions (which I shall henceforth call simply version one and version two) are interesting in a number of respects. There are both losses and gains, but it is clear that Dylan aims in version two at a more concrete simplicity. In the fifth stanza the phrase "walks along with a parrot that talks", which is oddly out of accord with the song's predominant cliché style and looks as if it had slipped in by mistake from *Blonde on Blonde*, is replaced by "walks along through the city blocks", which contributes to a more unified tone. The changes in verse four are rather different. To bring out their force it is necessary to quote each version in full:

1. He woke up, the room was bare
   He didn't see her anywhere
   He told himself he didn't care
   Pushed the window open wide
   Felt an emptiness inside
   To which he just could not relate
   Brought on by a simple twist of fate.

2. He woke up and she was gone
   He didn't see nothin' but the dawn

Got out of bed and put his clothes back on
Pushed back the blind
Found a note she'd left behind
But he could not concentrate
On anything 'cept a simple twist of fate.

The loss here is "told himself he didn't care", which is a clearly expressed and psychologically right observation (a cliché of feeling rather than of expression); the rest is mostly gain. Version one represents an attempt to render a feeling abstractly, and not a particularly successful one. It is scarcely clear precisely what is meant by not "relating" to a sensation of emptiness: the word has a slightly pretentious, intellectualised ring to it; while "brought on by" is simply clumsy. The only physical act in this version is the opening of the window. In version two, by contrast, everything is concrete and physical – a series of actions, with the sense of what the character is feeling left to be implied from what we are told of his behaviour. "He didn't see nothin' but the dawn" is clearly preferable to "He didn't see her anywhere" – it says the same thing indirectly and concretely instead of directly and abstractly. He sees the dawn, gets out of bed, dresses, pushes the blind back, finds and reads the note; we see him doing these things automatically, visualise his confusion, know that he does them because he can think of nothing else to do. Finally this feeling is focused in the one abstract phrase, which this time does sum up his state of mind: "he could not concentrate". The episode has been related by means of solid, visualised images.

The song is one of those which close with a summing-up verse, or *moralitas*, and this again is quite different in the two treatments. Dylan's aim is making the changes was probably broadly similar to that suggested for verse four, but this time the losses and gains are a little more evenly distributed:

1. People tell me it's a sin
   To know and feel too much within
   I still believe she was my twin
   But I lost the ring
   She was born in Spring
   But I was born too late
   Blame it on a simple twist of fate.

2. People tell me its a crime
   To remember her for too long a time
   She should have caught me in my prime
   She would have stayed with me
   'Stead of going back off to sea

And leaving me to meditate
Upon that simple twist of fate.

To me the first two lines here are clearly superior in version one.
The alternative is not unsatisfactory (and improved in the singing
by a light emphasis on the word "too"), but the original is sharper,
deeper, more moving – just the difference, in fact, between sin and
crime. The following two lines are good in both versions; but for
the last three, version two certainly has the edge. "She was born in
Spring / But I was born too late" is poetic, but it does not mean a
great deal: its significance seems rather esoteric, and it does not
follow from the content of the song as do the equivalent lines of
version two. "Going back off to sea" is an effective metaphor for
what we have been shown the woman actually doing, while
"leaving me to meditate..." is an accurate description of what
takes place in the song as a whole: it is a meditation on something
past and gone. So in making these changes Dylan is, once more,
working his way towards "the simplest way I can tell the story,
make this feeling real".

If any Dylan song looks cinematic, it must be 'Lily, Rosemary
and the Jack of Hearts'. Indeed Dylan at one time had plans, I
believe, to make it into a short movie. Yet it would surely present
major problems to any film-maker. It is conceived as a Western, and
has great dramatic panache, but its main intention seems to be to tell
a story which is *psychologically* convincing, to invest the stereotypes
of the convention with depth and with inner motivation. The ways
in which Dylan achieves this would not be easy to reproduce cine-
matically; and moreover, it is not at all clear what actually *happens* in
the song. It is almost as if Dylan were making the action intentionally confused and foggy in order to allow the characterisation to
stand out the more clearly – a reversal of the usual principles on
which Westerns are constructed. Commentators do not appear to
agree about even the central events of the story. *Bob Dylan – An Illustrated History* interprets it: "Down the street the Jack's gang was
cleaning out a bank, and in the cabaret, Big Jim shot the Jack...
Lily was left in the empty cabaret, thinking of ... the Jack of
Hearts, a murdered thief."[3] This is certainly wrong, and indeed
nobody else seems to read the story this way. The Jack is not shot by
Big Jim. The relevant verse runs:

No one knew the circumstance
But they say that it happened pretty quick
The door to the dressing room
Burst open and a cold revolver clicked
And Big Jim was standin' there
Ya couldn't say surprised

TELLING THE STORY

Rosemary right beside him
Steady in her eyes
She was with Big Jim
But she was leanin' to the Jack of Hearts

"A cold revolver clicked" is scarcely an appropriate way to describe the successful firing of a shot. Big Jim's gun has somehow been emptied, probably by Rosemary, possibly by Lily, or even – who knows? – by the Jack himself, the best actor around. (Verse four remarks that " . . . his bodyguard and silver cane / Were no match for the Jack of Hearts"). "Ya couldn't say surprised" is an understated way of saying that Big Jim is totally flabbergasted – by the failure of his gun to fire. Nor would Romemary be described as "leanin' to the Jack of Hearts" if by this time the Jack of Hearts was lying dead on the carpet. Rosemary then stabs Big Jim in the back with a penknife and is hanged for it the next day. The last we hear of the Jack is that he is not present at the hanging; not because he is dead – when Dylan sings "The only person on the scene / Missin' was the Jack of Hearts" the tone couldn't be described as elegiac – but because he has rejoined his gang and made off with the haul.

So much is clear. What is not so clear is *why* Big Jim tries to kill the Jack. In verse six he is uncertain of the latter's identity, thinking that he may have seen the face in Mexico or in a picture "up on somebody's shelf". At this point, then, he does not know that his girl-friend Lily is having an affair with the Jack of Hearts. Where he has seen the face before is, we may surmise, on a WANTED poster. It seems to make sense to suppose that Big Jim suddenly remembers this, and goes to kill the Jack as a wanted outlaw; but it is still not so simple. For in verse twelve, immediately before the catastrophe, as the Jack holds Lily in his arms in the dressing-room, it is "jealousy and fear" that he feels "beyond the door". There are two people beyond the door – Big Jim and his wife Rosemary. Do both emotions belong to Jim, or is either the jealousy or the fear – or are they both – emanating from Rosemary? Jim is going to the room of his mistress, after all, which could make Rosemary jealous; and he is going to shoot the Jack, to whom she is attracted, which could make her afraid for him. But it is more likely to be Big Jim who is jealous; while he would also have good reason to be afraid. At the end of verse six both Jim and the Jack are staring at Lily. Probably the former notices her attraction for the Jack and becomes suspicious when he disappears: it may be that his memory is thereby jolted into identifying the wanted man. I suggest that Big Jim tries to kill the Jack out of jealousy, but in the knowledge that he can do so with impunity because the man is an outlaw.

To complicate matters further, in the song as recorded on *Blood on the Tracks* Dylan omits the crucial verse twelve, in which the phrase "jealousy and fear" occurs, and which makes explicit the relationship between Lily and the Jack of Hearts:

> Lily's arms were locked around
> The man that she dearly loved to touch
> She forgot all about
> The man she couldn't stand who hounded her so much
> "I've missed you so" she said to him
> And he felt she was sincere
> But just beyond the door
> He felt jealousy and fear
> Just another night
> In the life of the Jack of Hearts

The song has sixteen verses and it is not surprising that one should have to be omitted on the recording for reasons of space; moreover, this is not a particularly striking stanza in terms of poetry. All the same, it is an odd one to miss out if the intelligibility of the train of events is regarded as important: on that count, the certainly more atmospheric verse eleven would be a more obvious candidate for omission. The conclusion can be drawn that Dylan likes to confuse his audience, likes to upset their expectations, and in so doing indicates what he considers to be important and what unimportant. On that reading, then, an understanding of the exact sequence of events is relatively immaterial: Dylan wants his song to work primarily in terms of its sensuous, dramatic and psychological impact. In this aim he is undoubtedly successful; when all is said and done we enjoy it most for its atmosphere, its immediacy, its swift flow of observation and movement, without caring too much about the details of the action.

As I hinted earlier, this emphasis turns on its head the central convention of the Western. In such a movie, the most dramatic action of the story – the slaying of Big Jim – would have occupied the centre of the stage. In the song, on the contrary, it occurs, as it were, off-stage, left merely to be inferred from subsequent developments, in the classic style of the ballad. We see Rosemary, "steady in her eyes", standing beside Big Jim but "leaning' to the Jack of Hearts"; at this crucial point the scene shifts to the gang completing the bank robbery and waiting "In the darkness by the river bed" for the Jack to complete his "business back in town" – his date with Lily. Now, with a consummate sense of drama, Dylan reveals the outcome of the scene he cut away from:

> The next day was hangin' day
> The sky was overcast and black

TELLING THE STORY

Big Jim lay covered
Killed by a penknife in the back
And Rosemary on the gallows
She didn't even blink . . .

He never does state explicitly that Rosemary killed her husband, far less show it happening.

Something else which we learn about only indirectly – insofar as we learn about it at all – is the character of the Jack himself. He is, of course, another stereotype from the mythology of the Western: the enigmatic and charismatic stranger who rides into town, accomplishes his shady business and rides out again, leaving all behind him altered, for good or ill. The trouble with such a figure is that when we see him in action, when his creator is obliged to show something of his character, his mystery and charisma are liable to turn out a cheat and a disappointment – they conceal a hollow. That is the point of the song 'John Wesley Harding', as Michael Gray has shown in one of the most impressive passages in his book.[4] So Dylan preserves the legend by never allowing us to see the Jack in action. In verse two he comes in, orders drinks for everyone, and asks what time the show begins; thereafter he does absolutely nothing that we can see except, in the omitted stanza (and this could be another reason for its omission) embrace Lily. Unlike the other three actors, who are each of them characterised in a brilliantly economical thumbnail sketch, the Jack is known to us *solely* through his impact on other people. After buying the drinks he moves into the corner "face down like the Jack of Hearts", preserving his anonymity and inviolability. Big Jim stares at him, lost in a trance; Lily has never met anyone like him; Rosemary gazes to the future, "Riding on" him, and later leans towards him; the gang can go no further without him; in the final scene he is notable by his very absence. The song ends with Lily thinking about him, riveted by his memory. In all this we learn nothing at all of what he is actually like. He is the still centre of the story, controlling the other actors by his very silence, inaction and passivity: precisely, in fact, as Dylan himself does in *Renaldo and Clara*.

The other characters, too, are stock figures: Big Jim who "owned the town's only diamond mine" (a typical passing flash of humour); Lily, the chorus girl with dyed hair and too much experience; Rosemary, the neglected wife of the great man; the drunken hanging judge. The first three, however, are individualised and made real in a remarkable way by the slightest of suggestions. As Big Jim stares over "into space" at the Jack of Hearts, seeming not to hear when Rosemary tries to speak to him, we get a sense of his brooding, jealous nature, the insecurity underneath the dandy exterior which

makes him rely on "his bodyguards and his silver cane" which are
to prove no match for the Jack of Hearts. Then when did we ever
learn in a Western about the childhood of a saloon girl? But Lily, we
are told, "was fair-skinned and precious as a child"; she "came away
from a broken home" and "had that certain flash everytime she
smiled". Already we feel that we know a lot about her and why she
behaves as she does, although in fact very little has been said. In the
case of Rosemary, Dylan manages to convey a considerable degree
of complexity in the character in only a few lines. When she first
appears "Lookin' like a queen without a crown", flutters her false
eyelashes and whispers in Big Jim's ear her apology for being late,
we understand how much she is in thrall to the husband who pays
her so little attention. The rest is said in verse nine:

> Rosemary started drinkin' hard
> And seein' her reflection in the knife
> She was tired of the attention
> Tired of playin' the role of Big Jim's wife
> She had done a lot of bad things
> Even once tried suicide
> Was lookin' to do just one good deed
> Before she died . . .

We all know the mood in which we gaze at our own distorted image
in the mirror of a knife: a bitter, drunken, deeply dissatisfied, self-
critical, dangerous mood. To encapsulate such a complex feeling in
a single, sharp, realistic image is a mark of what we can only call
genius in Dylan. Rosemary's situation is conveyed with the *ne plus
ultra* of economy. It is her disenchantment rubbing against her continued dependence on her husband, and thus giving rise to self-
hatred, which urges her on to the killing of Big Jim: the Jack of
Hearts merely provides the occasion. We can see, too, how jealous
resentment of Jim's affair with Lily plays its part: Rosemary is
drawn to the Jack, but no doubt she is also grateful to him for steal-
ing Big Jim's mistress. There is great irony, again, in the last four
lines quoted: while attempted suicide is not regarded by most
people as the worst of actions, Rosemary's "one good deed" (while
it does save someone) is destined to be murder.

The song is remarkable for the skill of its structure – about half-a-
dozen things are going on at any one time and Dylan never loses
control of any of them – and for the small, living details that allow
us to hear, see and smell what is going on: the "gentle breeze"
blowing in from the filling evening streets, the "brand-new coat of
paint" on the wall which Lily warns the Jack not to touch; the black
and overcast sky as Rosemary stands unblinking on the gallows.
The last verse provides the most revealing psychological touch of

all. The murder of Big Jim has caused Lily to think, perhaps for the first time in her life; she has even "taken all the dye out of her hair", surely not only because the cabaret is "Closed for repair"; but in the end her psyche is still dominated by the illogical, tyrannous primacy of sexual attraction:

> She was thinkin' 'bout her father
> Who she very rarely saw
> Thinkin' 'bout Rosemary
> And thinkin' about the law
> But most of all
> She was thinkin' 'bout the Jack of Hearts.

3

In considering the narrative songs on *Desire* we have to bear in mind that the lyrics in question were all written in conjunction with Jacques Levy. The collaboration seems to have been a close and immediately successful one, and Dylan has said that he can no longer "remember who wrote what".[5] It is therefore impossible to assign any particular aspect of the writing to either artist, and hard to speculate on what Levy's role may have been in the process of composition. If the lyrics are tighter in form and sentence structure than much of Dylan's earlier work, that only continues a tendency which was already observable in *Planet Waves* and *Blood on the Tracks*, and has been maintained since; it seems to have to do with his having learned how "to do consciously what I used to be able to do unconsciously", as he put it in an interview.[6] He attributes this development to the help of "a man in New York City who taught me how to see", who "put my mind and my hand and my eye together in a way that allowed me to do consciously what I unconsciously felt." There is no reason to suppose that he is referring here to Levy, whom he mentions a few sentences further on as his collaborator on *Desire*: it is *Blood on the Tracks* which he speaks of as the first fruits of the new way of seeing (and *that* album, to my ear, has much in common with its predecessor). The difference between unmediated instinct and feeling which has been modified by consciousness is what mainly distinguishes his first great period, 1965–66, from what for me at least is the second, beginning around 1975 and still, at the time of writing, continuing.

To most listeners, *Desire* seems in tone to be characteristic Dylan, much more characteristic for instance than anything between *Blonde on Blonde* and *Planet Waves*. Perhaps there is a tropical sunniness about much of it that we do not often associate with Dylan; and certainly Levy's contribution, whatever it may have been, ought not to

VOICE WITHOUT RESTRAINT

be diminished. As this is a book about Dylan, however, I hope that Mr Levy will forgive me if, for the sake of convenience, I allow the phrase "and Levy" to be understood in contexts where I refer to Dylan as author of the lyrics in question.

We have seen how Dylan often has pairs of songs on his albums, songs that look like twins but turn out to be much less alike at close quarters than they appear at first glance – "contrasting twins" we might indeed call them. One such pair is 'Hurricane' and 'Joey'. On the surface both appear to be songs championing the underdog, the victim of the law, the man who by force of his circumstances "never had a chance". Both are long, ballad-like numbers, interesting in their verse construction, and each opens a side of *Desire*. 'Hurricane', however, is in its content and attitude the most straightforward, uncomplicated and direct of all Dylan's narratives; 'Joey', as we shall see, is very different.

'Hurricane' is explicit in setting out to tell a true-life story:

> Here comes the story of the Hurricane
> The man the authorities came to blame
> For something that he never done . . .

A story with a moral, then: a story which sets out to right a wrong, which "won't be over till they clear his name / And give him back the time he's done". There seems no reason to doubt its sincerity as a contribution towards a practical aim, the securing of the reversal of the verdict against Rubin Carter and the quashing of his sentence. The mood is one of *saeva indignatio*, of contempt for the "authorities" and shame at living "in a land / Where justice is a game." Dylan means to tell it the way it happened (though Patty Valentine, for one, disagreed about that), and he plunges us straight into the action: "Pistol shots ring out in the bar room night". The outer structure is simple. The first seven stanzas recount the events leading up to the trial; the eighth focuses on the man himself, the victim; the ninth describes the trial and its outcome; the last two provide direct comment on the whole. Comment is, of course, implicit throughout the song, and at various points before the final verses it becomes explicit:

> In Paterson that's just the way things go
> If you're black you might as well not show up on the street
> 'Less you wanna draw the heat.

Subtler ways of putting the message across are also to be found. The police are allowed to condemn themselves out of their own mouths by the vulgarity and inappropriateness of their language: "Wait a minute, boys, this one's not dead"; "We want to put his ass in stir". We are able to look in on the processes of perversion of justice as the

68

cops are shown "puttin' the screws" on Arthur Dexter Bradley, one of the men the song presents as having been pressured into bearing false witness against Carter:

> "Remember that murder that happened in a bar?"
> "Remember you said you saw the getaway car?"
> "You think you'd like to play ball with the law?"
> "Think it mighta been that fighter that you saw runnin'
>   that night?"
> "Don't forget that you are white"

Here, interestingly, is a case where the printed word is able to put across something that cannot be fully communicated in the song as sung: the separate sets of inverted commas for each police question give us the full sense of the harrassment involved, two or more cops shooting questions at their victim in turn and in rapid succession, whereas the same passage sung sounds like a single speech or a general impression of the drift of the questioning (as is really the case in the next verse); the pace is too rapid to allow Dylan to differentiate adequately between two or more voices. Such methods, at any rate, work in conjunction with the full-blooded virulence of direct statement:

> All of Rubin's cards were marked in advance
> The trial was a pig-circus, he never had a chance . . .
>
> And though they could not produce the gun
> The D.A. said he was the one who did the deed
> And the all-white jury agreed

Carter himself is scarcely given any individuality, any characterisation beyond what is necessary to establish him as the object of injustice, one who was "falsely tried". In the lines where his professional role is referred to, there is a hint in Dylan's voice of the acknowledgement of an element of intentional cliché " . . . he never liked to talk about it all that much / It's my work, he'd say, I do it for pay . . ." But though this is a cliché it is also true, and that hint carries no irony over to make ambiguous the lines that follow:

> And when it's all over I'd just as soon go on my way
> Up to some paradise
> Where the trout streams flow and the air is nice
> And ride a horse along a trail
> But then they took him to the jail house
> Where they try to turn a man into a mouse

Dylan is not concerned here with injecting the kind of ironical overtones which would make of the song something "impartial" or "objective". The case is, both metaphorically and literally, a black-and-white one. Rubin Carter is a man whose life lies "in the palm of some fool's hand", "An innocent man in a living hell". To use such a subject as an occasion for any kind of irony would be grotesquely inappropriate.

Two lines at the beginning of the last stanza of 'Hurricane' may serve to open the discussion of its "contrasting twin", 'Joey':

> Now all the criminals in their coats and their ties
> Are free to drink martinis and watch the sun rise . . .

The contrast is, of course, with Rubin Carter, the innocent man condemned to sit "like Buddha in a ten-foot cell". Joey, the hero or anti-hero of the song that bears his name, also spends time in jail – ten years, in fact – and like Carter he is envisaged as a victim of the law, "hounded" by the police department, one of a clan of whom it is said that "It always seemed they got caught between / The mob and the men in blue". Unlike Carter, however, he really *is* a criminal: however dubious may be the grounds on which he is jailed, the act which leads to his death is the emptying of a register, which links him with the contemptible Bello and Bradley of 'Hurricane'. We are reminded of the 'criminals in their coats and their ties", too, by the lines which describe Joey after his release from jail:

> When they let him out in '71
> He'd lost a little weight
> But he dressed like Jimmy Cagney
> And I swear he did look great . . .

Joey, then, is as much a victim of his own self-image, and of his cultural inheritance, as he is a victim of the law. The latter, certainly, comes under Dylan's fire as unequivocally as it does in 'Hurricane'; the tone however is subtler, more sarcastic:

> The police department hounded him
> They called him Mr Smith
> They got him on conspiracy
> They were never sure who with
> "What time is it?" said the judge
> To Joey when they met
> "Five to ten," says Joey
> The judge says, "That's exactly what you get."

The venomous mockery of the way Dylan delivers that fourth line is unforgettable. Joey, however, is presented as something of a dumbwit, helpless before the judge's malicious cruelty. He is at once "King of the streets, child of clay", and the one may be taken as implying the other. In the last resort it is not the law which breaks

Joey, it is his own kind: he is blown down by another gangster in an act of vengeance brought on by his own rashness, pride and stupidity, the qualities that make his brothers call him "Crazy Joe".

When *Desire* first appeared Dylan seemed to some reviewers to be glorifying a hoodlum. It is true that Joey is the recipient of a large measure of the artist's *sympathy*, as one who has to live "in society / With a shackle on [his] hand"; and that he is given the credit for various good deeds or attitudes: stopping his associates from mur-dering some enemies who were held as hostages; "tryin' to stop a strike" in prison; refusing to carry a gun because he is "around too many children". His whole case, however, is from the start seen in the light of that characteristic irony which is so conspicuously withheld from that of the Hurricane. Unlike Carter he is in many ways more myth than individual. Born in Brooklyn in "the year of-a who knows when", he finds himself from the beginning "Always on the outside", but he doesn't know why; when asked, he can reply only "Just because". We get the impression of a happy, close-knit family, but there is an irony about this which can cut either way: the hoodlums are at the same time a happy family, but on the other hand this happy family are also hoodlums. A vagueness surrounds their activities: "Some say they lived off gambling / And running numbers too"; they are, naturally, always in trouble with the law:

> There was talk they killed their rivals
> But the truth was far from that
> No one ever knew for sure
> Where they were really at . . .

"The truth was far from that" – that is the kind of nebulous, indecisive phrase which is made by an apologist who cannot back up his assertion with evidence; and so little seems to be known about these people that we wonder how he can be so sure.

It is not, of course, Dylan who is speaking directly to us in his own person in this song, as he does in 'Hurricane'. He adopts instead the persona of a sympathetic observer, one close enough to Joey to be present at his funeral and, most important, one who belongs to his world and speaks his kind of language. The device allows the listener a perspective from which to *assess* what the narrator has to tell us about Joey and his life. The sordid gangland war is described, for instance, in almost heroic terms: "Joey and his brothers / Suffered terrible defeats", "they ventured out behind the lines / And took five prisoners". We are not, I think, meant to take a similar view of these activities. When Joey saves the threatened hostages from murder, disinterested love of humanity does not seem to rank high among his motives:

VOICE WITHOUT RESTRAINT

> But Joey stepped up, he raised his hand
> Said, "We're not those kind of men
> It's peace and quiet that we need
> To go back to work again"

It is his "work" with which he is primarily concerned, and we have at least an inkling of the nature of that. He spends his ten years in Attica "Reading Nietzsche and Wilhelm Reich", but as soon as he gets out he tries "to find the way back in / To the life he left behind" and demands "what's mine" from the boss. Even his pious refusal to carry a gun because the children he is "around", "should never know of one" has a sentimental, and on an uncharitable view a hypocritical, ring to it when we consider that his life-style has been built precisely upon the power of the gun. Moreover it is foolish, for having deprived himself of this only means of protection he continues with the way of life which depends on it, walking "right into the clubhouse / Of his life-long deadly foe" and emptying out the register. As in his youth, "Crazy Joe" still believes himself to be bullet-proof. To the question "What made them want to come and blow you away?" the obvious reply is that there could have been a whole lot of reasons. Joey is a gangster, one with some decent instincts certainly, but still a gangster, and he dies by the same code by which he has lived.

It is necessary to stress all this because the song as it is sung seems to present a more sympathetic picture of Joey, *in toto*, than can be found in what the words say; the music is melancholy and nostalgic in tone, giving the whole a certain elegiac quality, so that we may assume the sympathy to be less equivocal than it really is. "To sing praise to the King of those dead streets" may indeed, as the liner notes suggest, have been the impulse behind the writing of 'Joey', but the praise does not therefore have to be uncritical or unrealistic. Another sentence from the same source may be worth noting here: "Romance is taking over". Romance is an important element in *Desire*, and we may assume that the romance of the world of "those dead streets" is part of the feeling which Dylan is trying to put across in 'Joey'. This romance can be reached only from within. The mimicing of the accordion to whose sound the gangster opens up his eyes at the beginning of life tells us almost as much about the feel of that life (or the song's view of it) as we learn from the recounting of the events which make it up. A similar pathos surrounds his end. When "his best friend Frankie" is quoted as saying "He ain't dead, he's just asleep", Dylan sings the phrase in such a way – almost in a caressing manner – as to bring out both its cliché quality and the sincerity of feeling which it attempts to express. We are meant, I believe, to suspend our judgment here, and the scepticism which might ask how much of the town of Brooklyn really mourned Joey as we are told it did.

In the lines which follow, however, we are reminded of the standpoint from which the narrator is telling us of Joey's life and death:

> And someday if God's in heaven
> Overlookin' his preserve
> I hope the men that shot him down
> Will get what they deserve

God is thus imagined as just another gangland boss whose role it will be to avenge the deed that has been perpetrated in his territory, and thus to perpetuate the very circle of violence in which Joey was trapped. It is part of the authenticity by which the world of the dead streets is seen from the inside in this song, that not even in the final *moralitas* are its values transcended.

The quality of romance is even more marked in the three remaining songs on *Desire* with which we have to deal here. If 'Hurricane' is the most realistic and direct of Dylan's stories, the most surreal and allegorical is surely 'Isis'. It is a song dominated by an obsession, the narrator's obsession with a woman bearing the name of an Egyptian goddess who can be taken, to borrow a Dylan phrase from another context, "as literally or as metaphysically as you need to".[7] Of the mythical connotations it is probably enough to say that Isis was a nature goddess in ancient Egypt, with dominion over the earth and the seas, that she came to be an epitome of the Great Mother, and that she was confounded in later cultures with Aphrodite, the Greek goddess of love. All this may mean no more in the present context than that she is being used as a symbol of Woman; but she also functions in the song as a specific woman, with all the power which only specific women have to dominate the emotions of specific men and keep them hanging on. She is presumably responsible, besides, for the extraordinary hybrid topography of the song, which introduces the Pyramids into the North American far north, into Alaska or the Yukon.

'Isis' uses, once more, the balladic framing device, and in a way very similar to that of 'Tangled Up in Blue': the song is circular, starting with the narrator's departure from a woman, bringing him through an extended adventure, and returning him to the same woman at the end. No time is wasted in delineating the relationship at the outset, for Dylan sees the need to plunge straight into the action; only one essential feature is made clear:

> I married Isis on the fifth day of May,
> But I could not hold on to her very long.
> So I cut off my hair and I rode straight away

For the wild unknown country where I could not go wrong.

As well as establishing the narrator's position of weakness in his relations with Isis, and launching him on his journey, this first verse
introduces the song's religious symbolism. In cutting off his hair he
is shedding complexity: he sets off on a quest for simplicity of
living, seeking "the wild unknown country" where, according to
the American myth, issues are clear-cut and uncomplicated and
man's only struggle is with Nature. The irony is, of course, that in
the wilderness things go even worse for him than before.

That the quest is also a religious allegory is made clear by verse
two:

> I came to a high place of darkness and light.
> The dividing line ran through the centre of town.
> I hitched up my pony to a post on the right,
> Went into a laundry to wash my clothes down.

Thus far the narrator's expectations have not been disappointed:
right and wrong are clearly divided, and in hitching his pony to a
post "on the right" he opts for light rather than darkness. He then
continues, in the laundry, the ritual purification which began with
the cutting off of his hair. But from this point on everything goes
wrong: the outside world intrudes once more upon his illusion of
simplicity, in the shape of a stranger who approaches him and
makes him a mysterious offer which, it seems, he cannot refuse. Just
as the image of the "high place of darkness and light" represents
moral certainty, so does the stranger represent muddiness and confusion. It is not made clear what it is that they are after, and it soon
appears that the narrator is almost as much in the dark as we are. But
his obedience is unquestioning:

> We set out that night for the cold in the North.
> I have him my blanket, he gave me his word.
> I said, "Where are we goin'?" He said we'd be back
> by the fourth.
> I said, "That's the best news that I've ever heard."

We can see that in all ways our hero is getting the worst of the
bargain. He exchanges something real and invaluable, in the shape
of his blanket, for his partner's "word" on which he has no reason
to place trust (and his word about what?), and when he asks one
question he receives the answer to another which he has not asked.
In the face of uncertainty he takes the same supine and subservient
approach which marks his relations with Isis, who continues to dog
his thoughts more effectively than even gold and precious stones.
Like an expert storyteller Dylan makes use of the pause provided by

the journey, when nothing else is happening, to flesh out the picture of the relationship. The narrator is thinking as he rides:

> How she told me that one day we would meet up again,
> And things would be different the next time we wed,
> If I only could hang on and just be her friend.
> I still can't remember all the best things she said.

All the bitterness of his fully conscious slavery is contained in that last line, which Dylan delivers with a malevolent little hint of a laugh on the phrase "best things", a laugh which says that the only way he can maintain his self-respect is to assert his superiority over the woman by *knowing* her and placing her.

The expedition of the narrator and his partner combines the motif of the search for gold in the far north with that of the Egyptologist who breaks into the tomb of the mummy – the combination would make for a bizarre movie. As they reach "the pyramids all embedded in ice" the partner reveals that he is trying to find a body which should "bring a good price", which occasions the comment " 'Twas then that I knew what he had on his mind". Does this indicate that the narrator understands which particular body his partner is seeking? It could be a Pharaoh's, or just possibly that of Osiris, the brother and husband of Isis who was sealed alive in a casket by his enemy and rival Set, and which is the object of a protracted quest by Isis in the original myth. However that may be, the mission is to prove fruitless: the stranger dies, perhaps from exposure in the "outrageous" snow and cold, perhaps the victim of a curse on him who disturbs the tomb ("When he died I was hopin' that it wasn't contagious", the narrator observes genially), but the survivor presses on:

> I broke into the tomb, but the casket was empty.
> There was no jewels, no nothin', I felt I'd been had.
> When I saw that my partner was just bein' friendly
> When I took up his offer I must-a been mad.

Perhaps the metaphor is of a religious search which leads nowhere. The haziness that is associated with the figure of the partner is maintained to the end: in the last two lines quoted the first subordinate clause leads nowhere, seems not to connect with what follows it, and explains nothing.

In a strange substitution, the hero places the body in the empty tomb: he sets off in order to help bring a body out, and ends by putting one in instead. That done, he is quick to get back to essential business:

> I said a quick prayer and I felt satsified.

VOICE WITHOUT RESTRAINT

Then I rode back to find Isis just to tell her I love her.

One of the most memorable images of *Renaldo and Clara* is Dylan singing the last verses of the song, standing with his arms raised, crossed at the wrists beside his head and pressed convulsively against each other, expelling the words from deep within him and with awesome intensity. There is something archetypal about this wanderer's return, who rides in "from the East with the sun in my eyes" to find everything as he has left it, the woman treating him with the callous casualness to which he is no doubt accustomed, himself as enthusiastically in thrall to her as ever. The laconic dialogue between them encapsulates the kernel of the relation with almost impudent wit and assurance; the way that Dylan howls his despairing but accepting "yes" when she asks if he is going to stay is not easily forgotten. The final verse stands outside the narrative and completes the circle of the song. This time Isis is addressed directly:

> Isis, oh, Isis, you mystical child.
> What drives me to you is what drives me insane.
> I still can remember the way that you smiled
> On the fifth day of May in the drizzlin' rain.

The last line echoes the song's first; he has been through hell and back again, has gained nothing and learned nothing, and now finds himself once more in the very situation which drove him forth. We can visualise a nightmare-like eternal recurrence of this cyclic movement.

The element of romance in the next story is acknowledged in the title: 'Romance in Durango'. It exhibits in a remarkable degree Dylan's ability to project himself into an alien cultural experience and extract its essence: and he does this through an instinctive understanding of the nature and the power of stereotypes. 'Joey' enters thus into the world of the hoodlum, *Nashville Skyline* epitomises the country mood, and I suspect that something not essentially dissimilar happens in relation to fundamentalist Christianity in *Slow Train Coming*. 'Romance in Durango' makes use of the stereotypes – including the *musical* stereotypes – of Mexican mythology, in order to reach the feelings and the colours of the real communal experience to which they point. Simply by taking them seriously, by refusing to adopt towards them the attitude of the enlightened metropolitan who can see in them nothing but cliché, he rediscovers their meaning and avails himself of their continued resilience. Dylan can sometimes sneer but he never patronises.

The song bases its structure on a device which we saw used briefly in 'Isis' – the use of a journey to tell a story retrospectively. In this case the narrator looks forwards as well as back, creating a kind of phantom continuation of the story which is destined never to become reality. The only directly narrated action is the catastrophe of the last verse, and that is told dramatically and continuously, in the moment that it occurs. This technique makes for admirable narrative tightness and great dramatic intensity. The first four lines give us both the essentials of the situation from which the story is to be told – a man and his girl fleeing on horseback from the law – and the pervading atmosphere:

> Hot chili peppers in the blistering sun,
> Dust on my face and my cape.
> Me and Magdalena on the run,
> I think this time we shall escape.

Mood and narrative elements are balanced so unobtrusively that we do not think of distinguishing between them. The journey itself summons up the history and culture of the Mexican people and thus helps to invest the particular incident with the depth and the heroism which it might otherwise lack: "Past the Aztec ruins and the ghosts of our people. / Hoofbeats like castanets on stone". This leads naturally into the narrator's "dream of bells in the village steeple", a dream in which he sees "the bloody face of Ramon". The background to the flight is then narrated through a swift and typically cinematic flash-back:

> Was it me that shot him down in the cantina?
> Was it my hand that held the gun?
> Come, let us fly, my Magdalena,
> The dogs are barking and what's done is done.

The cultural setting has been established with such tact and sincerity (both lyrical and musical) that we do not feel inclined to smile at the stereotypes of the fight in the cantina, the tracker dogs, and others to come; and Dylan can execute a typical Mexican quaver on the *i*-sound of "cantina" without lapsing into parody. Our sympathy for the escaping couple is subtly built up and consolidated, not least by the chorus with its haunting Spanish lines, which looks forward to the end of the long journey through the desert.

As the first verse presents the immediate situation, and the second looks back at the cause of the flight, so the third directs our attention forward towards the happy outcome which the narrator envisages. They will sit in the shade and watch the bullfight, "drink tequila where our grandfathers stayed / When they rode with Villa into Toreon." With all the ceremony traditional to their people, the couple are to be married in the little church. Then there comes, in four lines additional to the verse structure as it holds in the other stanzas, one of those strange flashes which impart a further dimension, a kind of numinous depth into the sense of a ballad:

> The way is long but the end is near.
> Already the fiesta has begun.
> The face of God will appear
> With His serpent eyes of obsidian.

The reference, presumably, is to a mask or image of the serpent god that will be carried in the fiesta procession. But into the little idyll that has been evoked, the words introduce a discordant and sinister element; the God of the "serpent eyes" appears like a cruel and avenging spirit; the face of the evil destiny which hangs over the heads of the fated pair. The sense of foreboding which the image carries with it lends a new irony to the "*Dios nos vigila*" of the chorus which follows.

The fourth verse recalls us swiftly to the present, and in only eight brief lines relates for us the final events of this tragic romance through the direct speech of the narrator. We are not witness to the last act, which occurs only after the song has ended, though it is implied in the poignancy and longing of the final chorus; but we are in no doubt of the outcome. "Aim well, my little one", sings the hero, "We may not make it through the night." The song remains forever poised between our foreknowledge of the end and its enactment.

Like 'Lily, Rosemary and the Jack of Hearts', 'Black Diamond Bay' really requires Dylan to make it into a film for us to be quite clear about what is happening. In spite of the vividness of its scenes its topography is uncertain. Its locale is vaguely tropical – a volcanic island with palm trees and cranes. The desk clerk wears a fez, speaks sometimes in French and sometimes, as do the other characters, in contemporary American-English. This however is far from a major source of confusion: not so the movements and behaviour of the femal character – or characters. In the first verse "she" is "Up on the white veranda" in "a necktie and a Panama Hat", looking quite different from the photo on her passport. She "walks across the marble floor", is invited into the gambling room but "walks the other way". Next she passes the Greek, on the spiral staircase: he is on his way up to the second floor to commit suicide, so she is coming down. She mistakes him, for some obscure reason, for the Soviet Ambassador, and starts to speak to him, but he passes on. We lose her for a verse, in the course of which the lights go out; she has not been inactive during this interlude if we are to judge by verse four:

> The desk clerk heard the woman laugh
> As he looked around in the aftermath
> And the soldier got tough

He tried to grab the woman's hand
Said, "Here's a ring, it cost a grand." She said
"That ain't enough"
Then she ran upstairs to pack her bags
While a horse-drawn taxi
Waited at the curb...

She tries to rouse the Greek, who has now locked himself behind a
door with a "Do Not Disturb" sign in order to do away with
himself; she wants to speak to him of approaching danger, but he
tells her to go away and proceeds to hang himself from the chandel-
ier. In verse six, by which time the island is sinking, she is back on
the balcony, being told by a stranger that he loves her. She "sheds a
tear and then begins to pray", and we learn no more of her than that
her Panama hat has somehow survived the earthquake.

All this is confusing, to say the least, and especially the episode
with the soldier. We hear the woman laugh, but we do not know in
what tone. Is the soldier offering her the ring for services rendered,
or about to be rendered? Could she want it to help her escape, or is
he anxious to be helped to escape himself? Is it the impending catastrophe that causes her to beg the Greek, "Help, there's danger near,
please / Open up the door", or could she possibly be frightened of
the soldier? Might this even be another case in which we are dealing
with more than one woman?

The answers to these questions are perhaps finally unimportant.
What we can be fairly sure about, from the evidence of some of the
other songs we have discussed, is that the lack of clarity is intentional and serves a purpose. The pettiness and confused behaviour
of the human actors in this drama, the triviality of their pursuits, are
set against the implacable certainty of the elements, which will
sweep them and their concerns away for ever, leaving no more than
"a Panama hat / And a pair of old Greek shoes". The woman – and
we must suppose that this is her main role in the story – is the only
person in Black Diamond Bay who is aware of the approaching
danger, if in a tardy and ineffectual way; yet she must share precisely
the same fate as the Greek, who is so wrapped up in himself, like the
others, that he fails to notice that his suicide is about to be rendered a
superfluous act. The rest of the cast are brutishly unaware: the
"loser", intent only on winning, at last does so and breaks the bank
even as the island sinks into the sea; the soldier and the "tiny man"
are absorbed first in the sale of the ring and then with their thoughts
of "forbidden love", while the volcano erupts and the lava flows
down from the mountain to engulf them. With the desk clerk, the
blindness is complete:

But the desk clerk said
"It happens every day"
As the stars fell down and the fields burned away
On Black Diamond Bay.

In each verse it is the final couplet which points up the unthinking
frivolity of the characters in the hotel. In Thomas Hardy's great
poem 'During Wind and Rain' a precisely similar device is used: the
body of the verses depict scenes of happy activity, but the last line
(following a refrain which runs in alternate stanzas "Ah, no; the
years O!" and "Ah, no; the years, the years") in each case brings an
image of ominousness or decay: "How the sick leaves reel down in
throngs!" "See, the white storm-birds wing across!"; "And the
rotten rose is ript from the wall". It is only in the last verse that the
truth is made explicit:

They change to a high new house,
He, she, all of them – aye,
Clocks and carpets and chairs
    On the lawn all day,
And brightest things that are theirs . . .
    Ah, no; the years, the years . . .
Down their carved names the rain-drop ploughs.

In 'Black Diamond Bay' the images of foreboding become more
inescapable as the disaster comes closer: first "the last ship sails and
the moon fades away"; then "the storm clouds rise and the palm
branches sway"; soon "the rain beats down and the cranes fly
away". But inside the hotel the party goes on, as it did on board the
Titanic, until all is overtaken by chaos. The island is finally delivered
to destruction:

. . . the fire burns on and the smoke drifts away
From Black Diamond Bay.

Lethal unawareness, in the face of the clearest signs warning of
imminent catastrophe, is the theme of the song. In this respect it has
close affinities with 'Desolation Row', even though it imparts its
message in the form of a story where the earlier work used the
mosaic method, building up its meaning through a series of discrete
image-clusters. Both, however, conclude with a last verse in the
form of a coda, delivered in the first person, which comments on
what has gone before (in the case of 'Desolation Row', obliquely)
and allows us to see it from a fresh perspective. Whereas in 'Desolation Row', however, Dylan appears to speak in his own voice, or as
close to it as he ever comes in a song, in 'Black Diamond Bay' the
coda is put into the mouth of a persona whose unawareness mirrors

and outdoes that of the characters in the tale. This individual is the typical American man-in-the-street, sitting sprawled in front of his television set "In L. A. watchin' old Cronkite / On the Seven o' clock news" when he learns of the earthquake:

> Didn't seem like much was happening
> So I turned it off and
> Went to grab another beer
> Seems like every time you turn around
> There's another hard luck
> Story that you're gonna hear
> And there's really nothin'
> Anyone can say
> And I never did plan to go anyway
> To Black Diamond Bay.

Who can with honesty maintain that he has never thought like that, spoken like that? The character so accurately delineated in these lines connects both inwards, with the figures of the song, and outwards with ourselves, the hearers. He exhibits in his attitude the very habit of burying one's head in the sand, the same self-centred inertia, which dooms the people on the volcanic island, and at the same time tendencies which we can recognise in ourselves and our neighbours. His function therefore is to prevent us from dissociating ourselves from what the song is pointing to, to act as a link between *us* and *them*: and it is done with wit and lightness of touch and never a hint of preaching. It is one more example of how effective a vehicle the narrative song has become for the insights of Dylan's mature act.

Since *Desire*, unfortunately, this fruitful and fascinating genre has gone into abeyance. There is only one work on *Street-Legal* which it might be stretched to fit, and that is 'Changing of the Guards'. This song does in a sense tell a story, but it is an obscure and fragmentary tale whose beauty depends heavily on its rhythms and imagery and hardly at all on its surrealistic narrative-line: it is much better dealt with in a different context. The preoccupations which dominate *Slow Train Coming* to the exclusion of all else have not, so far, appeared to lend themselves to narrative treatment. It is to the origins of these preoccupations that we shall now turn.

Chapter Four

Hard Rain and Slow Trains

"Every conviction has its history" wrote Nietzsche in *The Anti-christ*, "its preliminary forms, its trials and errors: it *becomes* a conviction after *not* having been one for a long time, and after *scarcely* having been one for an even longer time." Bob Dylan's recent conversion to Christianity has caused much dismay among his staunch admirers, much astonishment, alarm, and initially even disbelief. Yet this conviction has an exceptionally long history, and one which can be traced, through the songs, back to the very beginnings of his artistic career. This chapter will attempt to trace that history, and suggest that its outcome, far from being surprising, was predictable and perhaps even inevitable.

That Dylan is in the most general sense a religious artist has for long been a commonplace, if not a cliché, of comment on his work. We all know that he has been constantly searching, experimenting, toying with a variety of religions and philosophies. An entire book – Stephen Pickering's aptly titled *Bob Dylan Approximately: A Portrait of the Jewish Poet in Search of God* – has been devoted to an unconvincing attempt to show that his songs can be understood only with the aid of a detailed knowledge of Jewish religious texts. Discoveries of God, statements of faith, mystical intuitions and so on have been attributed to him by a long line of commentators, on the strength of little tangible evidence. Certainly various religious or quasi-religious interests have influenced and coloured his work: drug-mysticism, Zen, Talmudic philosophy, more recently the Tarot. But a far more definite, substantial and constant thread runs through Dylan's spititual and intellectual history, one which places him squarely in the mainstream of the Judaeo-Christian tradition. This thread has two distinct but related strands: a consistent apocalyptic world-view, and a fascination (of a persistence which suggests an element of self-identification) with the figure of Christ. Through most of his career these strands run parallel, close together but separate; but in *Slow Train Coming*, with the adoption of Christianity, they come together and intertwine.

It should be stressed at the outset that what Dylan's work before 1979 reveals *is* a fascination with these religious matters rather than

82

any kind of commitment; also that it is something that has come and gone, disappearing at times and periodically resurfacing – almost like a chronic recurrent ailment that its victim would rather forget. In 1974 he told an interviewer: "Religion to me is a fleeting thing. Can't nail it down. It's in me and out of me."[1] He goes on to acknowledge that it has provided him with images, "but I don't know to what degree." However it is primarily from Dylan's songs that we must decide how important a theme religion has been to him. As D. H. Lawrence said, "Never trust the teller, trust the tale."

Consideration of the importance of these preoccupations to Dylan must begin by taking into account his Jewish background and his mid-Western American environment. An apocalyptic view of world-history is of course the principal common ground between Judaism and Christianity, in spite of the differences of application, and marks the latter as a derivative of the former. Norman Cohn, in his *The Pursuit of the Millennium*, has shown how Christian apocalyptic, developing from earlier Jewish versions, gave rise to the millenarian fantasies of the Middle Ages, and how "Originally all these prophecies were devices by which religious groups, at first Jewish and later Christian, consoled, fortified and asserted themselves when confronted by the threat or the reality of oppression."[2] Judaism and Christianity, especially in their eschatological aspects, were both religions of the oppressed, of the underdog, and their world-views essentially compensatory. Christianity represents a psychological as well as an historical consequence of Judaism, and involves a spiritualisation and a rendering "otherworldly" of its prophetic structure. The compensatory myth of the "Chosen People" is transferred from a racial to a spiritual élite, but the basic fantasies – the total destruction of the world order represented by the oppressors, and the subsequent triumph and ascendancy of the oppressed – remain unaltered in their essence. Dylan too, at various stages in his career, appears at once as the champion and spokesman of the oppressed and the advocate of spiritual aristocracy. These complementary roles, quite apart from their possible relation to personal psychology, arise naturally from a background of Jewish tradition and experience, and find a special and appropriate application within Christian mythology.

If Dylan's apocalypticism appears natural in one whose habits of mind were nurtured within the religious traditions of Judaism, his preoccupation with the personality and the fate of Jesus might seem less readily explicable in terms of his background. Such a concern would certainly be surprising in a metropolitan or urban North American Jew growing up in a predominantly Jewish environment (though an example of that is provided by Leonard Cohen). Dylan however emerged from a smalltown Mid-Western community where Jews were very much in a minority: so much so that when his father, Abraham Zimmerman, died in 1968 he was buried in Duluth because there was no Jewish cemetery in Hibbing. Moreover Dylan's first girl-friend, Echo Helstrom, is quoted by his biographer Anthony Scaduto as claiming that he appeared, in his teens, to be ashamed of his Jewishness and anxious to conceal it.[3] (It should be said here however that Dylan has several times denied that it mattered much to him one way or the other.[4]) A sense of being an outsider in a Christian community might well be reflected in an identification with Jesus, a Jew who became the God the Gentiles.

There seems also however to be a layer of identification that is more personal. We shall see this emerge from the songs, but it is also suggested by more than one remark made by Dylan over the years. "And look what they *did* to him," Scaduto quotes him as saying of Christ into a friend's tape recorder about 1965;[5] and in a 1978 interview he shows the same kind of interest. "Many people say that Christ lives inside them: Well, what does that mean?" he asks. "I've talked to many people whom Christ lives inside; I haven't met one who would want to trade places with Christ." He goes on to speculate that if Christ were to return today "He would have to be a leader, I suppose."[6]

From his childhood onwards Dylan immersed himself in American popular culture and music. The music of rural and urban America, both poor white and black, is in its turn steeped in Christian mythology of a fundamentalist cast, and this could scarcely have failed to impress itself deeply on his consciousness. His first musical hero, Little Richard, became a preacher; in his High School Yearbook Robert Zimmerman's ambition is given as being "To join Little Richard", an objective which may now be seen as doubly prophetic.

It is important, when thinking about the ways in which Dylan articulates religious themes in his songs, to bear in mind the Blues, work-song and gospel music background that is his primary musical inheritance. There are two opposite but vitally complementary strands in his use of language. One is the use of mythical or religious language to talk about everyday experience; the other is the use of everyday language to talk about the religious, the spiritual or the metaphysical. Much of Dylan's power and depth lies in his ability to unite these strands. His "street-style" direct talking, which derives from his Blues inheritance, yields immediacy, direct honesty, and the feeling of a modern and colloquial, distinctly American experience and flavour. In the other direction, again and again his artistic resonance and power lie in his success in cloaking the everyday and human – love affairs, arguments, personal problems, drugs, restlessness – in a highly mythical language which provides them with a metaphysical dimension. It can sometimes be hard to distinguish these strands: to decide whether a song is really concerned with a religious theme or is merely using religious language to deal with something quite immediate. Equally, a religious theme can be concealed by being articulated in the language of the streets.[7]

Dylan's career began at a time of acute public anxiety, when the long Cold War of the nineteen-fifties seemed, from moment to moment, to be in danger of becoming very hot indeed. His songs of the years 1961–63 are punctuated by references to "the next war" and "The Third World War", and this anxiety is a constant backcloth to everything he was doing in those days. There was indeed real reason to fear that a secular but none the less total destruction was imminent. 'It's a Hard Rain's A-Gonna Fall' was a personal response to the Cuban missile crisis of Autumn 1962. This was also the time of the rise of black consciousness; there was a potent sense in the air of rising aspirations on the part of oppressed groups, with prospects of violent assertions of long-denied rights. Apocalyptic and millennial fears and aspirations are never risible or ridiculous. If they were, they would not have exercised the power they have over the minds of men or exerted their strange fascination through successive generations. On the contrary, they answer to basic and constantly recurring human needs and anxieties. One of the first achievements of Dylan's genius was to renew and revitalise these age-old myths through the working of his poetic imagination, in a way which struck a deep and powerful chord in the collective consciousness of his own time.

Although he would often reject vociferously any role as a "spokesman", Dylan seems to have been aware from the first that he had this kind of relationship to the deepest feelings of his contemporaries, and conscious that it fell to him to give them expression. In one of the least known of his earliest songs, 'Train A-Travelin'' he uses the railroad imagery to which he was to return so often to announce this stance:

There's an iron train a-travelin' that's been a-rollin' through the
　　years,
With a firebox full of hatred and a furnace full of fears,
If you ever heard its sound or seen its blood-red broken frame,
Then you heard my voice a-singin' and you know my name.

Did you ever stop to wonder 'bout the hatred that it holds?
Did you ever see its passengers, its crazy mixed-up souls?
Did you ever start a-thinkin' that you gotta stop that train?
Then you heard my voice a-singin' and you know my name.

VOICE WITHOUT RESTRAINT

Another of these very early songs, 'Let Me Die in My Footsteps', explicitly links the fear of nuclear war with the prophecies of Biblical eschatology, and incidentally introduces an image which perhaps contains the germ of 'Blowin' in the Wind', the song that made him famous (the reference in the last line of what follows is of course to fall-out shelters):

> There's been rumors of wars and wars that have been
> The meaning of life has been lost in the wind
> And some people thinkin' that the end is close by
> 'Stead of learnin' to live they are learning to die.
> Let me die in my footsteps
> Before I go down under the ground.

'Blowin' in the Wind', though it belongs to the same set of pre-occupations, is not itself apocalyptic in outlook, owing its power rather to a principle which Dylan was later to annunciate in a poem from the group called *Some Other Kinds of Songs*:

> you ask me questions
> an' i say that every question
> if it's a truthful question
> can be answered by askin' it.

'It's a Hard Rain's a-Gonna Fall' is the first Dylan song to give imaginative form to a comprehensive apocalyptic vision. It however, instead of using the device of the unanswered question, employs a simple question-and-answer structure to pile up a succession of striking and sinister images which suggest the foreboding quality of a time which is radically out of joint: "a dozen dead oceans", "a black branch with blood that kept drippin'", "a newborn baby with wild wolves all around it", "a wave that could drown the whole world", "guns and sharp swords in the hands of young children", "a white man who walked a black dog".. Though they do not contain specific echoes of the New Testament, the ancestry of these images is certainly to be found in the prophetic "signs" of the Last Days which are to announce the Second Coming of Christ. The stance of the singer too is unmistakably prophetic:

> And I'll tell it and think it and speak it and breathe it,
> And reflect from the mountain so all souls can see it,
> Then I'll stand on the ocean until I start sinkin',
> But I'll know my song well before I start singin',
> And it's a hard, it's a hard, it's a hard, it's a hard,
> It's a hard rain's a-gonna fall.

The reiterated phrase, rendered by Dylan with fine expressive variation, drives the point home with relentless power. The continuing

importance to him of this song and its theme has since been underlined by his giving the title *Hard Rain* to his 1976 Rolling Thunder
Review concert album, although the song itself is not included on
the record.

When we turn to 'The Times They Are A-Changing' we are confronted by a deceptively simple-looking song which actually
embodies a quite complex shaping and restructuring of traditional
"found" elements and their integration and application within a
contemporary prophetic vision. The central idea is the millennial
theme of the reversal of fortune: the oppressors are to be brought
low and their victims raised up. Michael Gray finds that "the
language of the song is weak – imprecisely directed and conceived
too generally".[8] I think it may be agreed that its mood of optimism
is somewhat facile – Dylan, indeed, acknowledges this in his extraordinary *Budokan* treatment by once substituting "might" for
"will" – "the loser now *might* be later to win". All the same, I don't
think that the way the language *works* is imprecise. The argument
proceeds by means of two related ideas which are contained in familiar quotations. The first – "The old order changeth, yielding place
to new" – sounds Biblical but is actually from Tennyson's 'Morte
d'Arthur' in *Idylls of the King*. The second is of the words of Christ,
"But many that are first shall be last; and the last shall be first."[9] The
imagery, meanwhile, is provided in each verse by a single traditional element of much associative resonance.

To deal with the latter first, the first verse develops a primordial
image of destruction, that of the Flood: ". . . admit that the waters
around you have grown". In the second the prophetic note is
sounded as Dylan addresses the "writers and critics / Who proph-
esise with your pen", and the metaphor around which the verse
revolves is that of the Wheel of Fortune – "the wheel's still in spin".
The battle which is echoed in the third verse is a cosmic one, and the
windows and walls which it will rattle refer back to all the walls in
the Bible which fell, or will fall, to God and His servants. The controlling image of the next verse is that of the road, again a perennial
image of spiritual sojourning and particularly resonant in American
popular song. Finally comes the most potent symbol of all, "The
order", not just the order of our society but the World Order upon
which all life depends and which will tremble and dissolve when
Chaos is come again.

Within this ground of resonating imagery the evocative sentences
quoted above are refashioned and deployed. The economy with
which this is done is remarkable. Take the four words "The old
order changeth". The first element, "old", appears in the fourth
stanza in the words "Your old road is / Rapidly agin'". The second,
"order", contributes the equivalent lines in the final verse: "The

order is / Rapidly fadin'"; and the third, "changeth", of course provides the refrain that is common to all verses, "For the times they
are a-changin'". The same short phrase, then, the same idea para-
phrased, is put to work three times, without significant repetition, in
different contexts of imagery. The second part of the same sentence
is not neglected either, giving us "please get out of the new one" in
the fourth verse. A similar process occurs with the other quotation,
"But many that are first shall be last; and the last shall be first." A
preliminary paraphrase, or complementary idea, occurs in verse
two: "For the loser now / Will be later to win." This prepares for the
final verse which is worth quoting in full:

> The line it is drawn
> The curse it is cast
> The slow one now
> Will later be fast
> As the present now
> Will later be past
> The order is
> Rapidly fadin'.
> And the first one now
> Will later be last
> For the times they are a-changin'.

The simplicity of the words and their apparently casual sym-
metry conceal a careful structuring which operates to great effect.
The first line, with its suggestion of the writing on the wall at Bal-
shazzar's feast, accentuates the sense of fate which was introduced
into the song by the Wheel of Fortune theme in the second verse,
and is in its turn powerfully reinforced by the "curse" of the following line. Still without introducing the original words on which he is
working, and thus avoiding any sense of the derivative, Dylan now
gives us a new variant of the idea they express: "The slow one now /
Will later be fast". This in turn leads into a further development,
"As the present now / Will later be past". The introduction at this
point of this apparently platitudinous statement is in fact a master
stroke, undercutting any complacency, any sense of distance on the
part of the listener; for its implied corollary is that the future, in
which the reversal of fortune which is the theme of the song will
take place, will then be the present, as immediate and real as now seems
the present which will then be past. The contrast between present and
past is focused by the ending of three lines with the word "now",
each time preceded or followed, or both, by rhymes ending in
"-ast". The sense of insecurity induced by this menacing stress on
the present is now intensified by the most ominous and far-reaching
statement of all – "The order is / Rapidly fadin'". Finally the Bibli-

cal words which lie behind the whole argument are at last spoken out, almost as direct quotation, and the resultant shock of recognition clinches the cunningly, and at the same time very movingly contrived effect.

What, lastly, gives the song its inescapable if somewhat callow moral force is that these disturbing words, so redolent of the familiar imaginative projections of the deepest hopes and fears of countless generations, are addressed in the most direct way to the people – the writers and critics, the senators and congressmen, the mothers and fathers – of contemporary America. Any lingering sense that this is simply an immature and one-dimensional song should surely be dispelled by the astonishing recreation which Dylan achieves on his *Budokan* record. The song is one which has grown with its creator, grown too with the collective experience of his audience over the years, and has now acquired a finer and more mature meaning than it had when it was first sung.

It is especially obvious in the case of 'The Times They Are A-Changin'' that one of the things which makes possible the success of Dylan's apocalyptic songs as modern renewals of an immensely potent myth is the freedom to manipulate its elements, including Biblical material, as metaphors in the pursuit of his own personal vision, and in relation to contemporary events and preoccupations. Had he been tied to a more literal interpretation of the mythic symbols of the apocalyptic tradition, or to a more rigid application of these to modern reality, incapacitating restrictions would have been placed on his freedom to make instinctive connections. In short it is very doubtful whether these songs could have been written by a fundamentalist Christian. On the other hand it is equally doubtful whether they could have been written by someone who was not steeped in, and fixated upon, the religious tradition which gave rise to this world-view.

The remaining important song in the early apocalyptic group is 'When the Ship Comes In'. Though it begins and ends on more sinister notes, this is basically a joyful and celebratory song, painting a traditionally-inspired picture of the era of peace and harmony which will dawn with the rule of the saints on earth; and Dylan's singing beautifully communicates this generous spirit, which is not in fact one of his most characteristic tones. 'When the Ship Comes In' shows the fundamentally religious nature of Dylan's apocalypticism, for its vision (unlike that of so many songs of the "Which Side Are You On?" variety[10]) bears no conceivable relation to anything that might come about through even the most profound changes in the social order. The song may have been influenced by Brecht's 'Pirate Jenny', in which Jenny the hotel maid fantasises about revenge on her oppressors: a ship will come into the harbour one day, bombard the town to fragments but miraculously spare only the "filthy hotel" in which she works; men from the ship will put everyone in the town in irons, Jenny will condemn them all to death, and finally the vessel will vanish with her on board. Brecht's song however says nothing of the harmony of which Dylan sings, a truly cosmic one in which all nature, animate and inanimate, participates. Yet, as in the ultimate Biblical source, this harmony is prefigured by a cleansing storm, and the messianic ship is awaited in an atmosphere of foreboding:

> Oh the time will come up
> When the wind will stop
> And the breeze will cease to be breathin'.
> Like the stillness in the wind
> 'Fore the hurricane begins
> The hour when the ship comes in.

The chosen metaphor is maintained and extended with the sea imagery expressing the coming transfiguration of the natural order as the ship hits the shoreline and the mythical morning breaks; the fishes, the seagulls, and even "the rocks on the sand" join in the cosmic affirmation.

Yet this powerful myth is not allowed to escape from the function it is given here as a sublimation of the aims and aspirations that underlie contemporary struggles; for "the words that are used / For to get the ship confused / Will not be understood as they're spoken", and at the millennial hour, in contrast to the present reality of oppression, "the sun will respect / Every face on the deck". The song ends, moreover, with a celebration of the vengeance which will overtake the unrighteous. Dylan here remains faithful in every respect to the Biblical spirit. The disturbing quality of the prophetic vision is enhanced by Dylan's characteristic capacity for psychological inwardness: he is able to make us imagine, from within the skin, what it will be like "on that dreadful day":

> Oh the foes will rise
> With the sleep still in their eyes
> And they'll jerk from their beds and think they're dreamin'.
> But they'll pinch themselves and squeal
> And know that it's for real
> The hour when the ship comes in.

As in 'The Times They Are A-Changin'', Dylan leaves direct Biblical reference until the final lines, where it strikes with clinching force. And it is, significantly, with comparisons with two crucial triumphs in the heroic history of Dylan's people – the drowning of

"Pharaoh's tribe" in the Red Sea and David's slaying of Goliath –
that the song comes to an implacable close.

Similar in attitude to this conclusion, though this time the tone is
humorous, is an early song about the Day of Judgment, 'I'd Hate to
Be You on That Dreadful Day', which exhibits the same pitiless
insight into the helpless panic of one caught in a waking nightmare:

> You're gonna have to walk naked,
> Can't ride in no car.
> You're gonna let ev'rybody see
> Just what you are . . .

Indeed the song delivers a message that would be entirely in place in
Slow Train Coming:

> You're gonna yell and scream,
> "Don't anybody care?"
> You're gonna hear out a voice say,
> "Shoulda listened when you heard
>   the word down there."

Before leaving this group of songs it is perhaps worth commenting on an apparent paradox inherent in Dylan's adoption of
"popular" causes during the so-called "protest" era. In the millennial mythology which he exploited in the songs we have been considering, the Chosen People, whether racially or spiritually
regarded, have always been envisaged as a tiny minority; and
Dylan's subsequent development has revealed him as profoundly an
individualist, having little truck with the majority of his fellow
human beings: a man capable at times of great sympathies and
generosities, but also exhibiting often enough a strongly misanthropic element in his nature. The identification, in the songs of this
period, of the struggle of good against evil with that of the masses
against their oppressors might therefore seem contradictory; but at
bottom it is not so. Dylan at his best has always been the champion
of what, for want of a better phrase, we must call human values; and
although (in spite of the claims of much sentimental idealism)
human values cannot be said especially to reside in the masses, considered as a group, yet at certain times they may *symbolise* such
values – mainly by way of contrast with the corruption of the order
which oppresses them. Dylan, as we have already seen, is one of
those artists who more often than not assert their convictions in a
negative form, in terms of opposition. In this respect his adoption
of Christianity is an interesting departure; though the spirit of his
commitment, as evidenced in 'Slow Train Coming', may suggest
that the psychological pattern has not altered much.

The second main element in the religious content of Dylan's early songs can be more quickly dealt with. The various direct references to Jesus do not gather into an integrated vision such as we have been examining in the apocalyptic songs, but they do testify to the strength of the hold which the figure of Christ seems always to have exercised over Dylan's imagination. Already in the very early 'Long Ago, Far Away' there is a strong suggestion of self-identification:

> To preach of peace and brotherhood,
> Oh, what might be the cost!
> A man he did it long ago
> And they hung him on a cross.

It is noteworthy that Jesus, and sometimes too his antithesis Judas, seem on occasion to be invoked when the context does not particularly call for it; the 'Masters of War', for instance, are told that "Like Judas of old / You lie and deceive", and Dylan seems to take Christ's name in vain when he suggests in the same song that "Even Jesus would never / Forgive what you do." A similar idea is expressed with greater poetic power in 'With God on Our Side':

> In many a dark hour
> I've been thinkin' about this
> That Jesus Christ
> Was betrayed by a kiss
> But I can't think for you
> You'll have to decide
> Whether Judas Iscariot
> Had God on his side.

After *The Times They Are A-Changin'* L.P. overt Christian imagery ceases for a time to occupy a prominent position in Dylan's writing, though the odd reference continues to crop up. The religious preoccupation tends now towards a nature pantheism such as first finds magnificent expression in 'Lay Down Your Weary Tune' a song never officially recorded by Dylan but included by The Byrds on their album *Turn, Turn, Turn*. A similar kind of consciousness is given voice in songs like 'Chimes of Freedom', 'Mr Tambourine Man' and 'Gates of Eden', the drug experience increasingly contributing towards a "mystical" view of reality which engenders its own type of imagery. In 'Gates of Eden' a Biblical image is of course central to the song's structure, but it has a much less specific, more generalised function than similar metaphors in the earlier visionary songs. Most of the finest songs are now concerned with very immediate realities, whether the complexities of personal relationships, the ecstasies and nightmares of the inner world of drugs, or the surrounding corruption of contemporary society. There is however one song from the astonishingly creative

period from 1965–66 which embraces *Bringing It All Back Home,*
Highway 61 Revisited and *Blonde on Blonde,* in which these themes are
interlaced and controlled by an overall vision which is close to that
of Dylan's apocalyptic mood, and that is 'Desolation Row'.

This song has already been admirably examined by Michael
Gray,[11] but there are perhaps some additional points to be made
about the two verses which particularly enforce the vision we have
been discussing. The third verse follows an introduction which
establishes the atmosphere of dislocation, blind turmoil and potential violence which prevails in Desolation Row, with this:

> Now the moon is almost hidden
> The stars are beginning to hide
> The foretunetelling lady
> Has even taken all her things inside
> All except for Cain and Abel
> And the hunchback of Notre Dame
> Everybody is making love
> Or else expecting rain . . .

The first two lines indicate, of course, the time when the heavenly
bodies will be blotted out; and the ominousness is underlined by the
use of the active mood in "to hide". As well as contributing to the
exquisite balance of the verse, the turn of phrase suggests that the
stars themselves are moved to horror by what is to come; and the
suggestion is reinforced by the action of the fortunetelling lady who
"has *even* taken all her things inside" – her occupation is gone, for all
individual fortunes, it seems, are to be annihilated in a cosmic
diaster. Dylan's flat, unmelodic enunciation of the words "things
inside" here contributes wonderfully to the effect of menace. Meanwhile the mood which dominates in the Row is one of heedless frivolity, of sticking the head in the sand, here represented in the line
"Everybody is making love" – surely not so much a reference to the
sexual act as a prophetic glance forward to the essentially sentimental cult of uncritical gentleness – "make love, not war" – which was
soon to surface and which proved, indeed, to be evanescent and
ineffectual. The rain which the more clear-sighted are expecting and
which is already causing the carnival sky to cloud over is, presumably, the "hard rain" of which Dylan had already sung; and any
redemptive vision seems hollow and unreal, as for Ophelia in the
next verse, who in spite of having her eyes "fixed upon / Noah's
great rainbow" cannot prevent herself from constantly "peeking"
into the immediate reality of Desolation Row.

Michael Gray has already shown[12] how "the most striking evocation of impending catastrophe" is achieved by the one line in the

penultimate verse:

The *Titanic* sails at dawn.

It remains to add only how the disturbance we feel at the heedless blindness which prevails aboard the great sinking ship is heightened by the reference to the childish behaviour of two great poets: "Ezra Pound and T. S. Eliot / Fighting in the captain's tower". This might be a crack at the futility of modern poetry, but it could also suggest that even the most conscious are not immune from the tendency to turn a blind eye to impending disaster, preferring to fix their gaze on what they see:

> Between the windows of the sea
> Where lovely mermaids flow
> And nobody has to think too much
> About Desolation Row.

Dylan, on the contrary, appears to welcome the approaching wreck:

> Praise be to Nero's Neptune
> The *Titanic* sails at dawn . . .

Though "Nero's Neptune" sounds like the ship's evil angel, that invocation may, of course, be understood as being uttered by those who have placed their ultimate faith in the ill-fated vessel; it all depends on whether the words are taken as being spoken with or without hindsight. The ambiguity is probably intentional, an expression of a characteristic irony. Nero, at any rate, certainly has a specific significance here: he it was who fiddled while Rome burned. (It would be fascinating to know whether this reference to Nero, so satisfyingly right in its context, was inserted by conscious intent or thrown up by a subliminal association in the way demonstrated for Coleridge by Livingstone Lowes in *The Road to Xanadu*. It is worth mentioning that Dylan has made a special point in an interview of speaking up for the intuitive nature of genius. He takes issue with a statement reputedly made by the interviewer, Jonathan Cott: "A genius can't be a genius on instinct alone." "Well, I disagree," says Dylan. "I believe that instinct *is* what makes a genius a genius."[13] In critical analysis it must always be borne in mind that something may be "intended" without being intended *consciously*.)

'Desolation Row', however, is exceptional among the songs of its era in its summation of the earlier apocalyptic mood. It is in the songs of the *Basement Tapes* period (following on *Blonde on Blonde* though not released until 1975) that Dylan's religious preoccupations really begin to surface once more; in two songs in particular, and significantly these are the first and last songs in the order chosen for *Writings and Drawings*, flanking obscene nonsense songs and

94

cryptic little parables which anticipate *John Wesley Harding*. The first song is 'The Mighty Quinn' and the second 'Sign on the Cross'.

It is hard to say why Michael Gray should have described 'The Mighty Quinn' as possibly [Dylan's] most trivial song",[14] if "trivial" is to be understood as indicating a lack of serious content; for Quinn is certainly a Messiah figure, the mighty warrior at whose advent all will be made right. Like 'Desolation Row', but on a smaller scale, this song presents a picture of the corruption and dislocation of contemporary society and of the alienation and disquiet of many of those who have to live in it, especially the young. It may be, indeed, that the apparently rather odd first line:

> Ev'rybody's building the big ships and the boats,

refers us once more to the fate of the *Titanic*. The sensation of decay and grossness is rendered by powerful, nightmarish, almost nauseating images:

> I like to do just like the rest, I like my sugar sweet,
> But guarding fumes and making haste,
> It ain't my cup of meat.

Against this unnatural and disquieting background, the redemptive role of Quinn is made crystal-clear in every verse:

> Ev'rybody's in despair,
> Ev'ry girl and boy,
> But when Quinn the Eskimo gets here
> Ev'rybody's gonna jump for joy.

The animal kingdom too, represented by the pigeons which will "run to him", will respect the Eskimo as a father; the prevalence of worry and disturbance is to be dispelled by the coming of the longed-for redeemer. All this is clear enough: but what are we to make of the strange refrain which rounds off every stanza?

> Come all without, come all within,
> You'll not see nothing like the mighty Quinn.

It would be surprising if it meant nothing. I suggest that Dylan, in celebrating the promise of his Messiah, here addresses himself to both Gentile and Jew, or just possibly to those outside and inside the Christian revelation. Dylan himself appears in the final verse of the song as an inspired outsider, a kind of chameleon figure, clear-eyed and detached, looking in from the outside, all things to all men, and capable of taking on any role.

The other song, 'Sign on the Cross', is at first glance more straightforward, but like many of the numbers on the coming *John*

VOICE WITHOUT RESTRAINT

Wesley Harding it intentionally confuses by an obfuscating vagueness of language at crucial points. This technique, which can be more readily examined in relation to that album, seems designed to frustrate any facile attempts at interpretation. The central idea of the song however comes across clearly enough:

> Yes, but I know in my head
> That we're all so misled,
> And it's that ol' sign on the cross
> That worries me.
>
> Well, it's that old sign on the cross,
> Well, it's that old key to the kingdom,
> Well, it's that old sign on the cross
> Like you used to be.

Even within these simple lines submerged question marks are planted: why "in my head", which rather surprisingly suggests a purely cerebral basis for that disconcerting worry? Who is "you"? Still, the underlying motif is obviously worry, a nagging and disquieting worry about the cross and what it represents. Something is now becoming clearer. Behind Dylan's prophetic utterances of doom directed towards society lies fear, personal fear, fear about his own salvation. Now for the first time, instead of projecting that fear outwards in apocalyptic imagery, he begins to examine its source within his own consciousness. He begins to talk, harping away familiarly in the tone of a travelling preacher-man:

> Well, it seems to be the sign on the cross. Ev'ry day, ev'ry night, see the sign on the cross just layin' up on top of the hill. Yes, we thought it might have disappeared long ago, but I'm here to tell you, friends, that I'm afraid it's lyin' there still . . . the sign on the cross is the one thing you might need the most.

He suggests, too, in the final verse, that this worry may be a sign of strength rather than of weakness. The song has, as it is without doubt supposed to have, a disconcerting, unsettling effect. One obvious question occurs: why "the sign *on* the cross", not "of the cross"? There was only one sign *on* the cross that I know of, and it was this: THE KING OF THE JEWS.[15] I submit that Dylan is asking, and from a Jewish point of view, the question: Was this man really the Messiah?

2

Of all Dylan's albums prior to *Slow Train Coming*, the one most often spoke of in connection with religion is *John Wesley Harding*.

This is appropriate enough; its imagery is certainly religious, and in some cases so are its themes. What is much harder to understand is why it should so often have been taken as an expression of *faith* – unless religious concern and faith are to be regarded as synonymous. Anthony Scaduto, for instance, claims that *"John Wesley Harding* is infused with a belief in God . . . The album is Dylan's avowal of faith."[16] Steven Goldberg sees in the record "his solution to the seeming contradiction of vision and life", and finds that "the creative manifestations of a life infused with God, [it seems to be Scaduto who did the borrowing here] gentleness and compassion replace bitterness and cynicism. He has discovered that the realisation that life is not in vain can be attained only by an act of faith . . ."[17]

One almost wonders whether these writers have ever *listened* to *John Wesley Harding*, as opposed to having glanced at the words. Dylan's view of life is, I think, much more astringent, much more demanding, much more uncompromising than such readings imply. We now have the advantage of being able to compare 'Harding' with *Slow Train Coming*, and to know what faith really sounds like out of Dylan's mouth. The two albums are antitheses: the latter is in all senses passionate, sometimes unrestrainedly so, whereas the earlier record (except in 'All Along the Watchtower') is passionless and sceptical in spirit, cool, detached and ironical in tone. Which is to be preferred – in artistic or in spiritual terms – is another, and much more complicated question; but there is no doubt which represents faith. The comparison however is not necessary – one has only to listen to Dylan's voice on *John Wesley Harding*. While remaining highly expressive and showing exceptional agility of intonation, it is flat, calculatedly shallow in timbre, somehow disembodied. It sounds like the way he sings the word "lifelessness" in 'Desolation Row' – there is a deathlike quality about it. Nothing comes out of that voice that sounds anything at all like faith. Rather it communicates a strong sense of the reality of evil: but in a much less direct way than, for instance, The Rolling Stones' more or less contemporary 'Sympathy for the Devil' from their album *Beggar's Banquet*.

The dominant atmosphere of *John Wesley Harding* is of hollowness, emptiness, vagueness, insubstantiality; at moments it impresses the listener almost like the onset of a sickness. This mood of spiritual greyness, of failed aspirations, is pervasive and certainly intended, and it is not transmitted only through Dylan's voice and its spare musical backing – even the cover reflects it. Recurrently through the album there is a calculated imprecision of language, thought and meaning. *Pace* Scaduto, who interprets all these vague parables with breathtaking assurance, the whole seems deliberately constructed in such a way as strenuously to resist interpretation. Michael Gray has brilliantly analysed the "significant ambiguity" of the title song, its "empty centre", and the way in which this works in Dylan's exercise of revaluation.[18] This carefully fashioned emptiness appears again and again, starting with the jacket notes.

Dylan teases us at the very outset with three kings who offer three rival "keys" to the record's meaning – Faith, froth and Frank. Frank later agrees that the third king was right, and we can probably trust him. Faith, then, is ruled out from the start ("I don't believe so", the little story ends), and so is froth – there *is* some point to the whole exercise. But in keeping with the record which it introduces, the tale of the Three Kings is continually offering us apparent footholds which turn out to be untrustworthy; we are left with nothing substantial on which to rest. Frank seems to be identifiable with Dylan, and perhaps with Christ, as he is visited by three kings. His wife's name is Vera (Truth?) and she addresses Frank once as "Oh mighty thing!", which might echo 'The Mighty Quinn'. There is also a man called Terry Shute (Fall?) who makes a speech full of significant phrases which add up to nothing. The kings beg Frank to "open it up for us" – "Not too far but just far enough so's we can say we've been there." In reply Frank goes through a pantomime which ends in his punching his fist through a plate-glass window. Later the kings leave with their various infirmities mysteriously made good. Vera suggests to Frank that it would have been enough to have told them that he was a "moderate man", and the little fable peters out.

If, in pursuit of our key, we now follow Frank into 'The Ballad of Frankie Lee and Judas Priest', we shall probably emerge similarly flummoxed. The fable is too long to paraphrase and the exercise would prove unproductive; but what is first to be noticed is the unsettling oddness or pointlessness of much of the phraseology – words, sentences and allusions occur which are disconcerting in ways which are difficult to put one's finger on. They are perhaps not quite appropriate, or they refer to matters that are unexplained, or they contain references that have no apparent point. As the story approaches its conclusion the fogginess only grows thicker:

> No one tried to say a thing
> When they took him out in jest,
> Except, of course, the little neighbor boy
> Who carried him to rest.
> And he just walked along, alone,
> With his guilt so well concealed,
> And muttered underneath his breath,
> "Nothing is revealed."

None of this makes any real sense. Why that "of course" with reference to the little neighbor boy, whom we have never heard of before? How could he walk "along, alone" while he was carrying Frankie to rest, unless he was a really quite exceptionally strong little boy? What was the cause of his guilt which he kept "so well concealed"? Certainly he has the last word about the meaning of the song, with his "Nothing is revealed." The "moral of the story", as stated in the last verse, namely that "one should never be / Where one does not belong", scarcely seems to follow inevitably from the events described; or at least those events are very unlikely ones to choose as an illustration of such a moral. Nor does the consequence drawn from the moral actually follow from it in any logical way:

> So when you see your neighbor carryin' somethin'
> Help him with his load,
> And don't go mistaking Paradise
> For that home across the road.

Are those first two lines a half-concealed teasing reference to the little boy's prodigious load? And what Frankie in fact did was to mistake "that home across the road" for Paradise, which is something quite different – though that *may* just be bad grammar.

"Nothing is revealed" could well serve as the motto not just of this song but of the whole album. I think however that it refers not merely to the opacity of the fables themselves; or more precisely, that that opacity stands as a figure for something else. Before explaining what I mean by that it is necessary to demonstrate the opacity further.

Let us look at 'I Dreamed I Saw St Augustine.' Augustine, according to Scaduto, represents "the duality of man's nature."[19] Maybe he does, but the message doesn't exactly come across loud and clear. The picture Dylan paints of the saint in the first verse, "tearing through the quarters" (again, oddly chosen phraseology) armed with a blanket and a solid gold coat, is faintly ridiculous, and though the incongruity may be attributed to dream perception it is not lessened thereby. He is "Searching for the very souls / Whom already have been sold." Is the grammatical solecism merely that, or is it introduced for a purpose, presumably as a deliberate source of confusion? We might assume the former if Dylan did not do the same thing in 'I Pity the Poor Immigrant,' in this case following the "whom" clause with two others using the correct "who":

> That man whom with his fingers cheats
> And who lies with every breath,
> Who passionately hates his life,
> And likewise, fears his death.

Dylan has testified more than once to the *care* he took over the words of of *John Wesley Harding*. It seems to me at least possible that these peculiarities are intentional, and that the intention is to confuse and distract. We are at any rate told nothing about the sale of these souls – who sold them, to whom, or why.

> "Arise, arise," he cried so loud,
> In a voice without restraint,
> "Come out, ye gifted kings and queens
> And hear my sad complaint.
> No martyr is among ye now
> Whom we can call your own,
> So go on your way accordingly,
> But know you're not alone."

Once more, the information given is quite indefinite, and its elements are inconsequent. We do not know why kings and queens in particular are addressed, let alone gifted ones, or whether there might be a martyr among them whom they could *not* call their own. Why should they go on their way "accordingly", and who is with them if they are not alone? We are offered only vagueness, and to surmise leads us nowhere.

> I dreamed I saw St Augustine
> Alive with fiery breath,
> And I dreamed I was amongst the ones
> That put him out to death.
> Oh, I awoke in anger,
> So alone and terrified,
> I put my fingers against the glass
> And bowed my head and cried.

The most glaring anomaly here, though I have read no comment on it by any of the interpreters, is that in reality St Augustine was *not* a martyr, and no one did "put him out to death". Anything, of course, can happen in a dream, but this dream is usually presumed to have significant meaning. (What might possibly be relevant is that St Augustine was perhaps the first Christian thinker to see in the End of the World a figure for personal death.[20]) The singer's emotions on waking up are also strange: it is very difficult to be angry and terrified at the same time. The true "key", I think – and it is itself a negative one – is contained in the second last line, which stands in contrast to Frank's shattering of the window in "The Three Kings" (and to the fate of the Poor Immigrant's visions, which "must shatter like the glass"). For Dylan is here seeing "through a glass, darkly", and we are sharing that experience. The song, and I believe the album in general, is about *not knowing*, and the terror which that inspires. "You fail to understand," says the judge to the drifter in 'Drifter's Escape', "Why must you even try?" Only a "bolt of lightning" can save the drifter, just as meaning can only be attained by the shattering of the glass.

The technique of neutralising apparently meaningful lines which promise manifold significance by interspersing them with others which are incongruous, odd, inconsequent or nebulous can be demonstrated for several other songs, notably 'Dear Landlord' and 'The Wicked Messenger'. Yet it is remarkable to what degree the aura of pseudo-meaning has misled commentators. An example is Steven Goldberg's comment on the ending of 'Dear Landlord'.

> Dear landlord,
> Please don't dismiss my case.
> I'm not about to argue,
> I'm not about to move to no other place.
> Now, each of us has his own special gift
> And you know this was meant to be true,
> And if you don't underestimate me,
> I won't underestimate you.

Goldberg sees that as "a prayer for true compassion"![21] No doubt he was led on to this by the talk of soul and suffering in the earlier verses; but even without the confirmation provided by the tone of Dylan's voice on the recording, what the landlord (whoever he is) is being offered here, and in a spirit of detached realism, is clearly a *quid pro quo*. The tendency to see in *John Wesley Harding* what is simply not there has made poor prophets of many of its critics. "And there will be no more sad songs from this singer: not for a long time to come."[22] Thus Scaduto. Jon Landau, too felt that "the essentially adolescent quest for certain truths, static imagery, finality and the underlying hostile world view which allowed him to create his compelling but ultimately unsatisfying visions have been superseded."[23] Whether or not we agree with the judgment that the quest for ultimate certainties is "essentially adolescent", subsequent developments have shown that it was very far from having been superseded for Dylan by any relaxed relativism. Landau was closer to the truth than the "faith" advocates when he saw in 'Harding' "a Dylan who is more prepared than ever before to accept uncertainty";[24] but "accept" is the wrong word. Rather, Dylan is here *confronting* uncertainty, because at the moment he can see no other way of overcoming it.

Dylan's procedure in *John Wesley Harding* is predominantly intellectual, much more clinical and less feeling than in any of his earlier work. The exception (leaving aside for the moment 'Down Along the Cove' and 'I'll be Your Baby Tonight', which look forward to the 'Love is all there is' theme of *Nashville Skyline* and *New Morning*), is 'All Along the Watchtower'. This, significantly, has proved the most durable song on the album, and the only one which has achieved a permanent place in Dylan's repertoire. Here, Dylan lays bare the emotions of fear and foreboding which underlie all the rest. With its dialogue between the joker and the thief it begins like an allegory in the characteristic style of the record, but from the start it has a greater sense of immediacy, of personal urgency: "There's too much confusion, I can't get no relief." With the words "So let us not talk falsely now, the hour is getting late", we are once more in the familiar atmosphere of apocalyptic prophecy. The line is not, as it is often considered, simply an acknowledgement that time passes and Dylan is getting older. The following lines make that clear, which take their imagery from the twenty-first chapter of Isaiah which prophesies the fall of Babylon and the destruction of its graven images:

All along the watchtower, princes kept the view
While all the women came and went, barefoot servants, too.

Outside in the distance a wildcat did growl,
Two riders were approaching, the wind began to howl.

The masterly economy with which the chilling sense of foreboding is communicated here has already been the subject of much comment. The riders, while coming in straight from Isaiah, also arouse an association with the Four Horsemen of the Apocalypse. Particularly remarkable is the way in which the simple growl of the wildcat ("A lion" in Isaiah) transfers them from the ancient Middle East to the American West. "This is from the Mohave Desert"; so Dylan introduces the number on the *Budokan* album. Isaiah 21 begins: "The burden of the desert of the sea. As whirlwinds in the south pass through: so it cometh from the desert, from a terrible land." A "grievous vision" is revealed to the prophet: "My heart panted, fearfulness afflicted me: the night of my pleasure he has turned into fear unto me." Now here is Dylan in his 1978 *Rolling Stone* interview: "*John Wesley Harding* was a fearful album – just dealing with fear [laughing], but dealing with the devil in a fearful way, almost. All I wanted to do was to get the words right. It was courageous to do it because I could have *not* done it, too."[25]

"Nothing is revealed." The real subject of *John Wesley Harding* is the withholding of revelation, and the way Dylan communicates this and symbolises it is to withhold *his* meaning (or at least part of it) from us. Just as the seeker after religious truth is assailed by portentous signs and hints for which he is unable to find confirmation by any objective yardstick, so Dylan constructs an allegorical system which invites elucidation but in the end repels it. His parables do not describe "the fall and rebirth of one man – Bob Dylan",[26] but rather reflect that man's fruitless striving after objective truth. In *John Wesley Harding* Dylan searches for a religious solution, and not finding it, turns away, towards traditional certainties of a different kind – those of Nature, love, the family, the countryside – values which in American terms find their typical expression in country music.

The last two songs reflect that transition. "'If ye cannot bring good news, then don't bring any'", the Wicked Messenger has just been told, in words "Which opened up his heart". So Dylan immediately sets about giving us the good news:

> Down along the cove,
> I spied my true love comin' my way.

In its lyrics and its musical form 'Down Along the Cove' is a light-hearted blues number about the arrival of carefree love, but Dylan's voice tells a different story. He exploits it here in a manner as extraordinary as in any song I can think of, divorcing meaning from expression with every unexpected inflection and vocal turn. The tone, though light, is entirely detached, dispassionate and ironic. But the words do ring true:

> I say, "Lord, have mercy, mama,
> It sure is good to see you comin' today."

In the final song he decides to give himself to the new mood, to bury, for the time being, his fears and his doubts. "You don't have to worry any more", he sings, and seems to be addressing himself, "You don't have to be afraid." The *mocking*bird is going to sail away, and "that big fat moon is gonna shine like a spoon", perhaps in contrast to the almost-hidden moon of 'Desolation Row'. The feeling, indeed, is the very one which comes under such critical scrutiny in that song, the feeling of not wanting to know, not wanting to have to think about it; and it seems to come from spiritual exhaustion.

> Kick your shoes off, do not fear,
> Bring that bottle over here.
> I'll be your baby tonight.

The "night of pleasure" which, as for Isaiah, has been turned into fear, is to be turned back into pleasure again. The final line mirrors faithfully the psychological retreat.

3

This retreat is exemplified by *Nashville Skyline* and *Self Portrait*.

On the former, Dylan has said, "you had to read between the lines",[27] but what you read there is very much up to the individual — few decisive pointers are on offer. Dylan seems here to be pursuing a substitute faith, a set of ideals in which he does not really believe, distorting his artistic personality by willing a relaxation and a serenity which in the depths of him he does not feel. Enjoyable though the resultant music certainly is, it leads into a *cul-de-sac* — a *cul-de-sac* represented by *Self Portrait*. On that album 'Minstrel Boy' gives us Dylan "stuck on top of the hill" and "lonely still", begging for someone to throw him a coin "to save his soul". By his own testimony, he felt at this time that his creative development was at an end.[28] Yet in *New Morning*, released only four months after *Self Portrait*, the signs of renewal are already in evidence. 'Day of the Locusts' announces Dylan's joy at this rediscovery of himself:

> I glanced into the chamber where the judges were talking,
> Darkness was everywhere, it smelled like a tomb.
> I was ready to leave, I was already walkin',
> But the next time I looked there was light in the room.

'Went to See the Gypsy' harks back to the mood and imagery of *John Wesley Harding*. Dylan goes to see a gypsy "stayin' in a big hotel"; the gypsy seems glad to see him coming, but unsurprised; they exchange indecisive pleasantries. Dylan goes off to the lobby "to make a small call out", and there "a pretty dancing girl" advises him:

> "Go on back to see the gypsy.
> He can move you from the rear,
> Drive you from your fear,
> Bring you through the mirror.
> He did it in Las Vegas
> And he can do it here."

Again we have that recurrent "fear", and the metaphor of the resistant, obstructing glass which somehow has to be penetrated and gone beyond. Dylan takes the girl's advice, but though he finds the gypsy's door open the gypsy himself has gone, and so has the girl; he has to content himself with watching the sunrise. This may not be a wholly serious song but it could be saying that the only way forward for Dylan is through the pursuit of his religious obsession, however little the truth may seem to yield to his endeavours. It has been suggested that the gypsy is a phoney saviour or guru and that the reference to Las Vegas is intended to discredit him; but it could equally well be read: "If he can do it in Las Vegas, then he can do it anywhere."

Two more songs on the album reflect this continuing preoccu-

pation. 'Three Angels' tells of how these forgotten Christmas dec-
orations continue all day to blow their horns above the street while
beneath them an unceasing surreal parade from "this concrete world
full of souls" passes by, heedless and unaware.

> The angels play on their horns all day,
> The whole earth in progression seems to pass by.
> But does anyone hear the music they play,
> Does anyone even try?

At one level the song is admittedly a spoof, a send-up of many
moralising talking-songs and accompanied "poems" – the way
Dylan enunciates it makes that clear enough; but then he often aims
to parody a genre and at the same time say something through the
parody. Human unawareness is one of his perennial themes, so
there is no reason to doubt that the song is making a serious, if not
especially profound point.

'Father of Night', the last song on the album, is a simple and
direct hymn of praise to God the creator. It is basically pantheistic in
spirit, but seems at the end to address a more personal kind of God.
And Dylan interrupts the long silence between *New Morning* and
Planet Waves with 'Knockin' on Heaven's Door', where the onoma-
topoeic reiteration of Christ's metaphor for the religious quest is
put into the unlikely mouth of Sheriff Pat Garrett.

With *Planet Waves* begins a new and great period in which, as in
the songs of 1965–66, much of the subject matter is provided by the
joys, complications and agonies of personal relationships; love
songs and hate songs predominate, as we have seen. Within this
context Dylan's habit of identifying himself with Christ, of which
we have noted examples at the very outset of his career, reappears as
a function of the self-dramatisation which is the mode of the two
long confessional songs on *Blood on the Tracks*, 'Idiot Wind' and
'Shelter from the Storm'. There appears to be a recognition of an
element of conscious posing in such lines as "She walked up to me
so gracefully / And took my crown of thorns". The extent of the
self-identification – we might almost say its effrontery – may not in
itself advance Dylan's religious search very far, but it does help to
explain its obsessive nature. In 'Idiot Wind' Christ is seen (in lines
which mix Christian imagery with something from a quite different source) as one who suffered but won through in the end:

> There's a lone soldier on the cross
> Smoke pourin' out of a box-car door
> You didn't know it, you didn't think it could be done,
> In the final end he won the war
> After losin' every battle . . .

VOICE WITHOUT RESTRAINT

The compensatory function of the habit is very apparent there; but it would be wrong to imply that the religious concern in these songs is merely a matter of personal psychology. Behind the autobiographical references and the personal recriminations lies an implicit critique of society which carries with it, yet again, apocalyptic connotations. The "idiot wind" blows not only from the mouth of the woman addressed but "like a circle around my skull / From the Grand Coulee Dam to the Capitol". The lines quoted above are preceded by these, which bring with them another reminiscence of 'Desolation Row':

> I ran into the fortune teller
> Who said beware of lightning that might strike
> I haven't known peace and quiet
> For so long I can't remember what it's like...

As in *Macbeth*, values have been reversed: "What's good is bad, what's bad is good"; while blasphemy is enacted by the representative of Christ's church on earth: "The priest wore black on the seventh day", mourning the completion of God's creation instead of celebrating it.

'Shelter from the Storm' is littered with images of disillusion in the religious quest, even in a context which underlines the Christ-identification:

> In a little hilltop village
> They gambled for my clothes
> I bargained for salvation
> An' they gave me a lethal dose...

The predominant mood of this song is one of futility, and even the "One-eyed undertaker" (who may possibly be the Antichrist, portrayed in some Islamic traditions as one-eyed) "blows a futile horn". "Nothing really matters much, / It's doom alone that counts" sings Dylan fatalistically, and the song ends with a nostalgic longing for regression:

> If I could only turn back the clock
> To when God and her were born
> "Come in," she said, "I'll give you
> Shelter from the storm."

The refrain, with its metaphor expressing maternal protection from the assaults of harsh reality, reminds us of the theme of 'I'll Be Your Baby Tonight'; and one suspects that the "God" referred to here, and now apparently lost, was a temporary and comfortable substitute for the elusive object of Dylan's pursuit at the time of *John Wesley Harding*.

HARD RAIN AND SLOW TRAINS

Religious themes are present in *Desire* only much more obliquely, and it must be remembered that the lyrics of all but two of the songs on this album ('One More Cup of Coffee' and 'Sara') were written in collaboration with Jacques Levy, so that it is impossible to be confident in assigning any specific content solely to Dylan. 'Black Diamond Bay', at any rate, has a theme close to that of 'Desolation Row'. This narrative, as we have seen, tells how the denizens of an hotel in a holiday resort obliviously pursue their shady objectives, deaf and blind to the signs of approaching catastrophe, even as a volcano at last erupts and the whole island is destroyed by an earthquake:

> As the island slowly sank
> The loser finally broke the bank
> In the gambling room
> The dealer said
> "It's too late now
> You can take your money
> But I don't know how you'll
> Spend it in the tomb" . . .

That other haunting tale 'Isis' has all the marks of a spiritual allegory, with its "high place of darkness and light" where the narrator is lured to take part in a bizarre and indefinite quest which is to prove fruitless. However the only overt religious references on the record come in 'Oh, Sister', where the sister addressed is warned that "Our Father would not like the way that you act", and exhorted:

> And is our purpose not the same on this earth?
> To love and follow His direction.

In this song too appears the preoccupation with death which also figures prominently in *Street-Legal* and Dylan's 1978 interviews:

> Oh, Sister, when I come to knock on your door
> Don't turn away, you'll create sorrow.
> Time is an ocean but it ends at the shore.
> You may not see me tomorrow.

It is plausible, besides, to suppose that the "valley below" of 'One More Cup of Coffee' is the valley of the shadow of death.

With the benefit of hindsight it is tempting to see in *Street-Legal* much that prefigures the coming conversion to Christianity; but Dylan's imagery on this album is a strange and difficult as any he has created; speculation about possible meanings must be tentative and much remains obscure. The songs also contain some of his purest poetry. 'Changing of the Guards', for instance, very much requires to be seen on the page as well as heard, especially as the record's poor production leaves many of the words difficult to make out. The first song on the record, it begins with what sounds like a terse summary of Dylan's spiritual history during the "sixteen years" of his public career, "sixteen banners united over the field / Where the good shepherd grieves". Thereafter the song tells, in marvellously evocative language, a fractured and elusive tale which yields little to a search for connected meaning until the declarations of the last two verses:

> "Gentlemen," he said,
> "I don't need your organization. I've shined your shoes,
> I've moved your mountains and marked your cards.
> But Eden is burning. Either brace yourself for elimination
> Or else your hearts must have the courage for the changing
> of the guards."

Dylan appears here to be dissociating himself finally from society and asserting that only the most radical change of heart can save mankind in the face of the destruction of Eden, the earthly paradise. The song ends with another of his millennial visions:

> Peace will come
> With tranquility and splendor on the wheels of fire,
> But will bring us no reward than her false idols fall,
> And cruel death surrenders with its pale ghost retreating
> Between the King and the Queen of Swords.

The wheels of fire and the falling idols are familiar components here, but new to Dylan is the prophecy of the defeat of death, which (in spite of the accompanying Tarot imagery) has a strong Christian connotation and precludes any "secular" interpretation of this vision.

'New Pony' is a song which takes on possible new elements of meaning in the light of *Slow Train Coming*.

> Once I had a pony;
> Her name was Lucifer.

The song is certainly at one level about the business of discarding one woman and acquiring another, and the name "Lucifer" suggests that the first one was devilish; but it now looks as if Dylan may also be saying that he has been riding the devil's mount. Then there is that disquieting refrain sung in gospel style by the backing vocalists: "How much longer? How much longer? How much, how much, how much longer?" This could mean "How much longer can this go on?" or "How much longer do I have to wait?" or, perhaps, "How much longer have we got?" Actually it probably means all of these, and more. That it does not relate in any exact way to the words of the song makes it the more disturbing – it is like a nagging worry at the back of the mind, insistently trying to make its way to the front. It is possible that this refrain echoes the words of St Augustine at the time of his crisis of religious decision. J. F. Kermode coments: "Though certain of the end desired, he was 'at strife' with himself; the choices to be made were 'all meeting together in the same juncture of time'. He said within himself, 'Be it done now, be it done now'; but he still hesitated between fair and foul, and cried, 'How long? How long? Tomorrow and tomorrow?'"[29]

With 'Senor' we are on firmer ground, at least in places. It seems reasonable to assume that the Lord is being addressed here. The first verse carries a reminiscence of the fear of war which dominated so many of Dylan's earliest lyrics:

> Señor, Señor, do you know where we're headin'?
> Lincoln County Road, or Armageddon?
> Seems like I been down this way before.
> Is there any truth in that, Señor?

Like 'New Pony', this song, with its pleading questions, radiates an atmosphere of anxiety and impatience: "How long must I keep my eyes glued to the door?"

> Señor, Señor, I can see that painted wagon.
> I can smell the tail of the dragon.
> Can't stand the suspense any more.
> Can you tell me who to contact here, Señor?

Could the painted wagon belong to that slow train which Dylan is soon to glimpse coming round the bend? The dragon whose tail he can smell probably comes from Revelation: certainly it is menacing and sinister, and in the panic of suspense he looks wildly around for help.

> Well, the last thing I remember before I stripped and kneeled
> Was that trainload of fools bogged down in a magnetic field.
> A Gypsy with a broken flag and a flashing ring
> Said, "Son, this ain't a dream no more; it's the real thing."

The first line is clearly an image of submission. Dylan is stripping himself of his defences and about to kneel down before God. The trainload of fools, surely, is another metaphor for the blind masses who, like the passengers on the *Titanic*, disport themselves in a fool's paradise even as they are carried onwards towards disaster. These fools take their place in the literary tradition of folly which has its origins in Sebastian Brant's *Narrenschiff* ('Ship of Fools') of

1494. The Gypsy, too, we have met before: he is the one Dylan went to see and who, he was told, could "drive you from your fear". The last line of the verse reminds us of something more: the foes who "will pinch themselves and squeal / And know that it's for real / The hour when the ship comes in." Dylan's long religious dream, the song seems to be saying, is about to become reality.

As Dylan now begs for a minute to pick himself up off the floor, and then announces, "I'm ready when you are, Señor", the impression is reinforced that he is preparing himself, gathering himself together, under the pressure of unbearable fear and suspense, for the decisive act of submission and for the advent of grace. The song ends with a plea for destruction (perhaps of the restraining inhibitions of his own mind), and a final gesture of impatience:

> Señor, Señor, let's disconnect these cables,
> Overturn these tables.
> This place don't make sense to me no more.
> Can you tell me what we're waiting for, Señor?

The word "Señor" gives us the stance from which Dylan is speaking. As the sub-title 'Tales of Yankee Power' indicates, the song is put in the mouth of the oppressed. The persona adopted enacts the attitude of submissive, almost cringing, but at the same time insinuating humility; but 'Señor' is not, as one reviewer took it to be, about "the plight of the Chicano".[30] True, Dylan's art often functions at a number of different levels, but the religious level is surely here much the deepest and the most passionately felt.

The Dylan of *Street-Level* is in a state of turmoil and often close to despair. In 'No Time to Think' we find him radically disillusioned with society and self:

> You can't find no salvation – you have no expectations
> Anytime, anyplace, anywhere...

but two verses later there is a strong hint of coming change:

> Starlight in the East, and you're finally released.
> You're stranded, but with nothing to share.

'Where Are You Tonight?' shows him physically exhausted and worn out by internal strife:

> I fought with my twin, that enemy within,
> Till both of us fell by the way.
> Horseplay and disease is killing me by degrees
> While the law looks the other way.

In the face of this sense of breakdown the last verse of the song looks forward to "a pathway that leads up to the stars", and "a new day at dawn". The form which this further 'New Morning' was to take should perhaps not have come as a surprise to us.

4

In the light of the religious history we have been surveying we can well understand the force for Dylan of the words from 'Precious Angel' on *Slow Train Coming*: "The enemy is subtle. How be it we are so deceived / When the truth's in our hearts and we still don't believe?" On this album he really does believe: or so it *almost* always appears. The commitment is startling in intensity when we consider the detachment with which Dylan was discussing religion with *Playboy* in March 1978, not much more than a year before.[31] He did condemn what he considered the irresponsibility of *Time* magazine in printing, a few years previously, a big cover-headline "IS GOD DEAD?": "I mean, if you were God, how would you like to see that written about yourself? You know, I think the country's gone downhill since that day." He felt it to be "pretty self-deluding" to think that there was nothing more than "the journey from point A to point Z" of human life. But he was very far from expressing any more committed religious position. "I'm not a patriot to any creed," he remarked. "I believe in all of them and none of them." When asked about his "sense of God" he replied, "I feel a heartfelt God. I don't particularly think that God wants me thinking about Him all the time. I think that would be a tremendous burden on Him, you know." On *Slow Train Coming* he exhibits no such reluctance to burden God with his thoughts.

The metaphor of the slow train is not a new one in Dylan's writing. It appeared previously, three times in all, on the jacket notes for *Highway 61 Revisited*; indeed this cryptic piece of writing opens with it: "On the slow train time does not interfere, . ." Later, "while the universe is erupting", Autumn "points to the slow train & prays for rain and for time to interfere –". It is singled out, finally, as one of the record's themes: ". . . the subject-matter – though meaningless as it is – has something to do with the beautiful strangers . . . the beautiful strangers, Vivaldi's green jacket and the holy slow train".

In the title song from the new album, as a matter of fact, the metaphor lacks the evocative power which it possessed in the earlier contexts, just because we know precisely what it stands for here – this train carries the Second Coming of Christ, the Millennium, the Last Judgment, the complete eschatological framework of the Christian faith. As a visual image it is very powerful but as a metaphor it lacks flexibility, open-endedness, complexity of resonance; unlike for instance Dylan's own "hard rain", which, though it carried mani-

fold traditional resonances and drew much of its strength there-
from, still came from a *personal* vision, was not tied to an exact and
specific meaning, and was therefore capable of change and growth.
This tells us something important about Dylan's treatment of the religious theme on *Slow Train Coming*. Because the threat expressed is
now felt as affecting others rather than himself, the emotional attitude towards apocalypse is very different from that of the songs of
the early sixties. The sense of menace and foreboding, of numinous
horror, can still indeed appear:

> Can they imagine the darkness that will fall from on high
> When men will beg God to kill them and they won't be
>   able to die?

but most of the passionate feeling is otherwise directed.

Though Dylan's apocalypticism might seem finally to come into
its own in a song like 'When He Returns', the strength of such a
song actually lies elsewhere. He is here responding to a vision which
is *given*, and that he has received; the artisitic interest and achievement lie less in the vision expressed than in his psychological and
emotional response to it – lie precisely in his struggle to accommodate himself to a vision *not* his own, which means for Dylan a
struggle for humility and self-effacement. Out of this struggle come
a number of songs of great intensity and emotional power.

Slow Train Coming is in some senses the kind of record we might
expect from a newly-converted Dylan: not at all simplistic, but at
the same time quite uncompromising: "Ya either got faith or ya got
unbelief, and there ain't no neutral ground." The songs divide
themselves into two principal groups: those, like 'Gotta Serve
Somebody', 'Slow Train', and 'When You Gonna Wake Up', in
which Dylan directs his energies to lacerating indictments of contemporary society set against a straight-forward religious alternative; and those in which he is primarily concerned with the impact
of his beliefs on his own consciousness, personality and conduct.
These songs are 'Precious Angel', 'I Believe in You' and 'When He
Returns', and they make the deepest impression, and the more
lasting one. Occupying an interemediate position are 'Gonna
Change my Way of Thinking' and 'Do Right to Me Baby', which
generally resemble the latter group in their overt stance but the
former in their underlying mood. 'Man Gave Names to All the
Animals', finally, is a lighter, witty number on a theme from
Genesis – a song that might have been written for children but
carries a sting in its serpentine tail.

The first group of songs harks back to the mood of Dylan's very
earliest work. While the fury is more comprehensive than in the
"protest" days, there is the same dichotomy between the corruption

of the world and an ideal order, though the latter is no longer seen as having any this-worldly application (except a literally millennial one). There is also a similar callow directness, with a thinness of imagery which has been uncharacteristic for Dylan since even the songs in which he was bidding farewell to protest, like 'My Back Pages' and 'It's Alright, Ma'. Thus although the mood of 'No Time to Think' on *Street-Legal* is developed there is a striking break with its method, which depended on very complex and difficult patterns of imagery. Dylan is of course an imcomparably maturer craftsman than he was when he was writing songs like 'Masters of War'. The wit and incisiveness of his vindictive critique of society's ills is often remarkable. But as Alastair Clark put it in a review of the album, "Oh, yes, it's lovely stuff. Whether it is the stuff of love is another question."[32]

> They talk about a life of brotherly love.
> Show me someone who knows how to live it . . .

sings Dylan in 'Slow Train', yet he shows little enough of it himself. Christianity, in fact, provides him here with a sanctioned outlet for his inveterate misanthropy. Always the champion of spiritual aristocracy, he paradoxically uses the religion of the underdog as a way of maintaining his own apartness, his inviolate integrity:

> Don't let me change my heart.
> Keep me set apart
> From all the plans they do pursue.

One of the less likable aspects of the record is the attitude of superiority which he adopts towards his "companions" who are still "unbelievers" and his "so-called friends" who have "fallen under a spell". Another is the offensively redneck philosophy which crops up here and there:

> Sheiks walkin' around like kings,
> Wearing fancy jewels and nose rings,
> Deciding America's future from Amsterdam and Paris.

In a sense Dylan has always been a traditional American patriot, and the above may actually be less inconsistent than it appears at first glance. All the same, becoming a "patriot" to a creed seems to have carried in its wake a more strident kind of national patriotism than he has previously given voice to.

The analysis of decadence, often just and accurate, at times breaks down into petulance, and this is reflected in some of the refrains which come round too often and with a tiresome insistence that is no doubt intentional: "When you gonna wake up?/When you gonna wake up?/When you gonna wake up?/And strengthen the things that remain?" Yet we must bear in mind that Dylan has always had a need to discover and define his positives in opposition to some external enemy. He recognised this clearly himself in the jacket notes he wrote for *Joan Baez in Concert Part 2* around 1963:

> An' I locked myself an' lost the key
> An' let the symbols take their shape
> An' form a foe for me t' fight
> T' lash my tongue an' rebel against
> An' spit at strong with vomit words . . .

This need seems to be a recurrent one, and when it comes Dylan gives himself to it, "Fearing not that I'd become my enemy / In the instant that I preach" ('My Back Pages').

'Do Right to Me Baby' is a song with many points of interest, giving expression once more to Dylan's disgust at the world but also revealing much about himself and his attitudes to his new beliefs. In structure it is not unlike 'All I Really Want to Do', presenting his state of mind through an accumulation of active and passive negatives:

> Don't wanna judge nobody;
> Don't wanna be judged.
> Don't wanna touch nobody;
> Don't wanna be touched.
> Don't wanna hurt nobody;
> Don't wanna be hurt.
> Don't wanna treat nobody
> Like they was dirt.

All this says something about the spirit of negativism which is in evidence in some of the more jaundiced parts of the record where he is, in fact, judging people constantly; but even more intriguing is the structure of the chorus.

> But if you do right to me, baby,
> I'll do right to you, too.
> Ya got to do unto others
> Like you'd have them, like you'd have them, do unto you.

Dylan here uses Christ's admonition as the basis of a deal he is offering his woman, applying it to her instead of to himself! This extraordinary reversal of the spirit of the precept can scarcely be accidental. Either he is guilty here of a most uncharacteristic moral obtuseness; or else, much more likely, his essentially subversive spirit is already at work (probably in spite of himself) on the moral foundations of his new-found faith.

Before his conversion Dylan had expressed the view that it is

"The fact that it was such a tragedy" that attracted people to Christ.[33] Doubtless he was speaking at least in part for himself, and it is not surprising that the concern with Christ's physical suffering should now surface once more:

> Stripes on your shoulders,
> Stripes on your back and on your hands.
> Swords piercing your side,
> Blood and water flowing through the land.

He empathises with Christ, identifies with his hurt, his loneliness and his persecution. The strongest songs, ironically, are those in which Dylan is most prepared to admit his own weakness, his uncertainties and his anxieties; and typically, when he does so he does it unequivocally. Even in 'Gonna Change my Way of Thinking', outwardly one of the most self-confident statements on the album, there is a suggestion that an attraction of religious faith is its offer of a refuge from the conditions of life, of "shelter from the storm":

> There's a Kingdom called Heaven,
> A place where there is no pain of birth ...

In songs like 'Precious Angel' and 'I Believe in You', Dylan gives the impression of still feeling his way around in his new spiritual surroundings. He is aware – as he seems not to be, for instance, in 'Slow Train' – of where he has just come from; how could I know you would be the one? he asks his woman,

> To show me I was blinded,
> To show me I was gone,
> How weak was the foundation
> I was standing upon.

Nor is he unwilling to admit present dependency:

> Shine your light, shine your light on me,
> Ya know I just can't make it by myself.
> I'm a little too blind to see.

Though in the printed version "can't" has become "couldn't", this is not the language of conventional religious "assurance". 'I Believe in You' and 'When He Returns' are at once the most passionate and convinced songs on the album, the most honest and giving of self, and – probably for that very reason – also the most tentative, uncertain, questioning. Dylan is now confident enough to admit his own vulnerability and need for help:

> Don't let me drift too far,
> Keep me where you are,

115

Where I will always be renewed.

'I Believe in You' starts out from an emotion which he has always felt intensely – self-pity, in this case because his friends are deserting him, turning him away because of his beliefs (listen to the passionate dramatisation of the first "I" in the words "And I, I walk out on my own . . ."). But the strength of the feeling rapidly transcends, and indeed consumes, the claims of the ego. The attitude of submission, the stripping away of pride, is something quite new for Dylan, and even without the moving intensity of his singing there is no mistaking the genuineness in the words:

> I believe in you when winter turn to summer.
> I believe in you when white turn to black.
> I believe in you even though I be outnumbered.
> Oh, though the earth may shake me.
> Oh, though my friends forsake me.
> Oh, even that couldn't make me go back.

An important ambiguity in this song must however be noted. There are lines in which Dylan appears to be addressing not God the Father or Son so much as a human lover (if indeed the distinction can properly be made – it is after all a common enough translation in the history of religious literature):

> I believe in you even through the tears and the laughter.
> I believe in you even though we be apart.
> I believe in you even on the morning after . . .

Finally, perhaps, it is his own *self*-belief that he celebrates:

> I don't mind the pain
> Don't mind the driving rain
> I know I will sustain
> 'Cause I believe in you.

What makes these songs so powerful is that they are still the products of a dynamic struggle with self, rather than static monuments to unalterable conviction.

'When He Returns' is a song of impassioned commitment in belief: "Truth is an arrow, and the gate is narrow that it passes through". (We are reminded of 'Restless Farewell': "But if the arrow is straight / And the point is slick, / It can pierce through dust no matter how thick.") It marks the continuity of Dylan's present beliefs with his perennial apocalyptic and millenarian obsessions:

> The strongest wall will crumble and fall to a mighty God.

. . . . . .

Like a thief in the night, He'll replace wrong with right
When He Returns.

It also, however, lays bare the psychological roots of these themes.
In words which echo and expand that disquieting background
refrain from 'New Pony', Dylan asks "How long can I stay drunk
on fear out in the wilderness?"; and, in a matching verse which
makes one of those sudden witches of person which are among his
most moving effects: "How long can you hate yourself for the
weakness you conceal?" We remember that, by Dylan's own evidence, fear was the subject of *John Wesley Harding*. Almost the last
words on the record seem to glance back over the religious history
which we have been tracing in his songs from the very beginnings
of his development. They are set out in a form which in the end
sounds like a statement but is actually a question, one of those truth-
ful questions which, as Dylan said so long ago, can be answered by
asking them:

> Can I cast it aside, all this loyalty and this pride?
> Will I ever learn
> That there'll be no peace, that the war won't cease
> Until He returns?

In the same passage from *The Antichrist* with which we began this
chapter, Nietzsche wrote this: "Conviction as a *means*: many things
are attained only by means of a conviction. Great passion uses and
uses up convictions, it does not succumb to them – it knows itself
sovereign." Our knowledge of Dylan's personality and of his spiritual and artistic history might suggest that his Christian conviction
is performing for him the kind of function of which Nietzsche
speaks. In recent years he seems to have passed through a period of
emotional and creative intensity comparable to his experience of
1965–66, after which he began seriously searching for religious sol-
utions, and, not finding them, retreated behind a protective barrier
of traditional verities. Such a retrenchment answers to that instinct
of self-preservation which a great artist must know when to culti-
vate, protecting the self's integrity by confining it for a time within
a received and restraining framework. Such a course Dylan may
now once more be instinctively adopting. If that is so one must hope
that a corresponding instinct will make him alive to the possible
dangers; dangers which are perhaps best suggested by these lines
from 'Visions of Johanna':

Inside the museums, Infinity goes up on trial
Voices echo this is what salvation must be like after a while . . .

What "salvation" meant for Dylan at that time was stasis, the end of development and of the need for development, the flux of living experience being exchanged for a reality no longer subject to change, with the fixed and permanent status of an object in a museum. It must be acknowledged that a religious conversion, by altering or obviating the psychological basis of the creative drive, may radically change the nature of an artist's endeavours, or even bring them to an end with a "lethal dose" of salvation. "You really just have to believe," Scaduto quotes Dylan as saying back in 1965, "And that's a dangerous business, just believing. You have to sacrifice a lot."[34] Just how much he will be prepared to sacrifice remains to be seen. Certainly he has now reached a place towards which he seems always to have been moving. He has been knocking on Heaven's door for a long time now; if it has at last been opened unto him we should not grudge him that. What happens to his art may depend less on his beliefs themselves than on the drives that lie behind them. As he has said himself, "You fail only when you let death creep in and take over a part of your life that should be alive."[35]

Chapter Five

Some Other Kinds of Poems

One of the favourite classifications used by journalists in their attempts to categorise Dylan has been that of the "poet". An article called "The genius who went underground", printed in the *Chicago Tribune* in 1967,[1] is a typical case in point. The writer tells how "Dylan is looked upon as a practising member of the craft" by "bearded guru poet Allen Ginsberg", Kenneth Rexroth, Robert Creeley and others. The tone attributed to these luminaries is embarrassingly patronising: Ginsberg, for instance, informs us that "He writes better poetry than I did at his age", while Michael McClure ("author of the controversial play, *The Beard*") is said to have called 'Gates of Eden' "the key to his completing a set of poems." It is perhaps fair to point out that the poets concerned were probably less responsible for this tone than the journalist quoting them. The whole piece has the true journalistic stench, with Dylan being offered to the man-in-the street for approval as endorsed by the mystic authority of "poets" (in the same way that "doctors say that..." and "scientists believe that..."), even though most of these poets couldn't hold a candle to him. The nadir of this "poet" preoccupation is probably reached in Johnny Cash's well-meaning but excruciating tribute on the jacket of *Nashville Skyline:*

> Here-in is a hell of a poet.
> And lots of other things
> And lots of other things.

Dylan has given his view of this classification of himself in an interview,[2] and typically he went straight to the point which the *Chicago Tribune*'s poets missed. In response to the question, "Do you consider yourself primarily a poet?" he replied: "No. We have our ideas about poets ... I don't call myself a poet because I don't like the word. I'm a trapeze artist." Ellen Willis is useful here with a comment which can serve as a gloss on Dylan's own: "When critics call Dylan a poet they really mean a visionary. Because the poet is the paradigmatic seer it is conventional to talk about the film poet, the jazz poet. Dylan is verbal, which makes the label even more

119

tempting. But it evades an important truth – the new visionaries are not poets."[3]

This does not, all the same, exhaust the argument. In another context Dylan acknowledges what people mean by the attribution when, on the cover notes to *Bringing It All Back Home*, he writes, "A poem is a naked person . . . some people say that I am a poet." Then again, he has written poems, and published them. Not only that, he has published his lyrics up to 1970 in a volume without the music, and included as illustrations in the hardback edition of *Writings and Drawings* some examples of his rough drafts, which show his methods of lyric composition to be not strikingly different from those of many poets. There are aspects of Dylan's song writing which will yield to critical analysis almost as if we were dealing with poems: Michael Gray's work on his language and imagery makes that clear. Dylan's lyrics are composed in writing, after all; in that sense he is not an oral artist. His art is a hybrid thing, influenced by poetry and other literary forms as well as by a profusion of musical traditions; and sometimes there are internal conflicts between its different aspects. This chapter will attempt to do two things: first, take some notice of Dylan's early poems, whose virtues seem to have been largely overlooked, and then consider certain aspects of the construction of his song lyrics which show a variable tension between the demands of the music and the look and feel of the words on the page. That Dylan is first and foremost a song writer is obvious; but there *are* some senses in which he is also a poet, and in which, I suspect, he thinks of his writing as being analogous to the writing of poems.

We have seen again and again that Dylan conceives his art as being a matter of giving embodiment to feelings in such a way that they can be experienced as real by his audience, felt anew by others. Ezra Pound said once that "The poet's job is to define and yet again define", and we can say that for Dylan making a song or a poem is a process of defining a feeling in as immediate and concrete a form as he is able to give it. The method of reaching this goal which he chooses in the poems that he was writing contemporaneously with his very early albums is that of accretion, the building-up of a sense of life from an accumulation of small particulars. That he was already able to convey a feeling in song lyrics with great economy is clear from such numbers as 'Girl from the North Country' and 'One Too Many Mornings', but his approach in the poems is utterly different. Here he uses the line-break entirely as a device for separating discrete impressions, attributes or experiences – there is almost never a run-on of sense from line to line:

Hibbing's got the biggest open pit ore mine in the world

SOME OTHER KINDS OF POEMS

Hibbing's got schools, churches, grocery stores an' a jail
It's got high school football games an' a movie house
Hibbing's got souped-up cars runnin' full blast on a Friday night
Hibbing's got corner bars with polka bands...

'My Life in a Stolen Moment' goes on to build up a picture of
Dylan's experience in the same way that it builds an impression of
his home town, by adding detail to detail in a succession of "atmospheric" images. The principle of one idea to a line is strictly adhered
to, and when the idea is physically too big for a line of print the unit
is nonetheless maintained in the way the words are set out:

I looked up a long time friend in Sioux Falls an' was let down,
    worried blind, and hit hard by seein' how little we had to say
I rolled back to Kansas, Iowa, Minnesota, lookin' up
    ol' time pals an' first-run gals an' I was beginnin'
    to find out that my road an' their road
    is two different kinds a roads...

The method is saved from monotony by switches of focus – from
places to people to experiences to influences and back to places
again. It is a device seen in its most extreme form in 'Last Thoughts
on Woody Guthrie', where it is underlined by the use of rhyme
(mainly couplets, though with some variation) and by the habit of
beginning line after line with the same word – "And" or "When",
for instance – in successive series of accretions from an initial
thought or image. The poem centres on two lines near the middle,
consisting of an almost meaningless phrase which is repeated in
such a way that the first half of the poem leads up to it and the
second expands away from it again:

    And you need something special
    Yeah, you need something special all right...

The first part tell us how you feel when you need it (that second
"need" is in fact the poem's first main verb), and the second what it
is that you need (it turns out to be God or Woody Guthrie, take your
pick, and the poem ends with the rather trite thought that both may
be found "in the Grand Canyon / At sundown."). This naïve construction is the excuse for assembling an impressive array of vivid
images which in accumulation really do succeed in giving substance
to a number of feelings that would otherwise remain vague and
diffuse:

And there's somethin' on yer mind that you wanna be saying
That somebody someplace oughta be hearin'
But it's trapped in yer tongue and sealed in yer head
And it bothers you badly when you're layin' in bed

And no matter how hard you try you just can't say it
And yer scared to yer soul you just might forget it
And yer eyes get swimmy from the tears in yer head
And yer pillows of feathers turn to blankets of lead . . .

In this poem the apparent point – the needing of "something special" – is little more than a hook for yoking together a scatter of disparate impressions. The much more successful 'Joan Baez in Concert Part 2' notes, by contrast, have a real and strong idea at their core, and the poem is genuinely exploratory. It takes as a starting-point a striking picture, that of Dylan as a boy kneeling beside the railroad line near his aunt's house as he waits for the "iron ore cars" to roll by, yanking the grass out of the ground and ripping "savagely at its roots". When the train has passed he looks at his green-stained hands and sees that he has "taken an' not given in return". This image provides him with a grip on what he wants to say about the way he was then and is now:

An' I walked my road like a frightened fox
An' I sung my song like a demon child
With a kick an' a curse
From inside my mother's womb – .

As he grows up he learns to intellectualise his instincts and impulses; he finds symbols to represent what he wants to fight and idols "T' be my voice an' tell my tale". His first idol is Hank Williams because he sang about the railroad lines, which symbolised reality to the boy. He comes to see beauty only in what is ugly, for only the ugly is real to him, and to reject everything that is conventionally beautiful. (Years later he was to tell an interviewer that "I see beauty where other people don't."[4])

Dylan describes how as he develops the symbol "beauty" continues to represent for him something to be resisted, how he shouts:

"The voice t' speak for me an' mine
Is the hard filthy gutter sound
For it's only this that I can touch
An' the only beauty I can feel" . . .

Then he meets Joan Baez and hears her sing, and for the first time is confronted by the need to ask himself whether there can be a value in the kinds of beauty which hitherto he has rejected. Asked about this poem by his *Playboy* interviewer in 1978, Dylan commented: "I was very hung up on Joan at the time. [Pause] I think I was just trying to tell myself I wasn't hung up on her."[5] That is no doubt true, and it is honest of Dylan to say so; but the poem itself gives form to a very much more intricate kind of honesty, a slow and painstaking analysis of the acquiring of a certain self-knowledge. It is something that could not have been done in a song, and indicates what sort of function the writing of these poems must have had for him at that stage in his career. It gave him the opportunity to stand back from himself and look coolly at his past and at his present situation, providing a different kind of outlet from the inspired immediacy that characterises his songs. Dylan is thinking here not instinctively but contemplatively, trying to get certain things clear through detachment rather than through the swift stab of insight. The effect is slower, more careful than that of the songs, and just because of that contrast the exercise is especially valuable, telling us much about the inner drives that forged Dylan's achievements in his major mode. It shows, too, that his success is not due to instinct alone, though instinct comes first. He has also thought about himself, criticised himself and modified his understanding as a result. The poem ends by returning to the image of the torn grass:

> I'll bend down an' count the strands a grass
> But one thing that's bound t' be
> Is that, instead a pullin' at the earth
> I'll jus' pet it as a friend . . .

What the poem does is to show, concretely, how realities give rise to feelings, which in their turn engender ideas; how these ideas can ossify and become rigid when divorced from their origins; and how eventually fresh experience, with the new feelings and emotions which stem from it, mounts an assault on the old ideas, and finally modifies or dissolves them. Dylan is always on the hunt of reality, trying to pin it down, but at the same time allow it its livingness, its dynamic. In this poem he does his work with patience and honesty, and with the help of much effective – and sometimes ambiguous – imagery:

> For the breeze I heard in a young girl's breath
> Proved true as sex an' womanhood
> An' deep as the lowest depths a death
> An' as strong as the weakest winds that blow . . .

The '11 Outlined Epitaphs' have a more "literary" feel to them. They have shorter lines, are more impressionistic and less direct in their approach than the earlier poems, and a few of them are obscure in places. They also show a number of definite literary influences: numbers three and four, for example, contain references to, or echoes of, Villon, Rimbaud and Eliot. The title indicates a certain provisional quality which sometimes shows through. The best of them however have again the purpose of commenting on Dylan's development and present situation, clarifying certain experiences for him in ways which were not available to him through the medium of song. In the second, for instance, he returns once more to his roots in an eloquent evocation of Hibbing which is at once a leavetaking of his early youth and a coming to terms with it. The fourth epitaph similarly looks back at his education and the decisive point at which he turned away from it, "not carin' no more / what people knew about things / but rather how they felt about things"; the sixth bids farewell to his "last idol", Woody Guthrie, who "just carried a book of Man / an' gave it t' me t' read awhile." All have, as might be expected, a certain valedictory quality: Dylan faces a nagging, troublesome idea and by giving it concrete and exact form is able to dismiss it and put it behind him.

Many of these ideas are thrust upon him from without; they represent the accusations and misunderstandings suffered by an artist in the public eye who is the eternal victim of comment and interrogation ("I am on the side a them hurt feelings / plunged on by unsensitive hammers"). The resulting apologias are the reverse of apologetic. The eighth epitaph, evidently an answer to accusations of plagiarism, magnificently overturns the false idea of artistic "originality", with a sharp and convincing analysis of the way an artist makes use of old material:

> t' make new sounds out of old sounds
> an' new words out of old words
> an' not t' worry about new rules
> for they ain't been made yet
> an' t' shout my singin' mind
> knowin' that it is me an' my kind
> that will make those rules . . .

In fifty-odd lines he says all that needs to be said on the subject and is able to bury it. The following epitaph performs a similar office for the magazine interview, for the journalists who complain when he fails to co-operate with them in presenting a picture of himself that will satisfy people "who want t'see / the boy nex' door":

> I don't like t' be stuck in print
> Starin' out at cavity minds . . .

A few lines of dialogue deftly present the kind of implied threat, the submerged blackmail which is used in an attempt to pressurise him into conforming. The exposure of those who seek to "expose" Dylan (which, he points out, he does himself "every time I step out / on the stage") is complete and unanswerable.

The last set of poems which Dylan allowed to be published in *Writings and Drawings* were those called 'Some Other Kinds of Songs'. They are, indeed, closer to his songs than the earlier poems, and closer too to the material and approach of his novel *Tarantula*. Some of them read like sketches for what he does more tightly and succinctly in the songs; and the beginning of the first could almost be from a discarded draft of 'Subterranean Homesick Blues':

> baby black's
> been had
> ain't bad
> smokestacked
> chicken shacked
> dressed in black
> silver monkey
> on her back . . .

These poems are less linear than those which went before, contemplative passages being interspersed with impressionistic anecdotes and little thumbnail sketches. Sometimes they are loosely linked by a recurring motif such as that of the man threatening to jump off Brooklyn Bridge; in general the ideas are less sharply focused than in the 'Epitaphs' or the Joan Baez concert notes. But they can be included with those poems in adding up to a picture of what Wordsworth, in his sub-title to *The Prelude*, called 'The Growth of a Poet's Mind'. We may presume that Dylan stopped writing these poems, or at least publishing them, when he felt sufficiently confident in his primary activity of song writing no longer to need to explain himself to himself or to others.

2

Before turning once more to the songs it is as well to remind ourselves that the distinction between song and poetry would not be readily understood by the people of many, if not most, cultures, including that of medieval Europe. Song form was the only form for lyric poetry throughout most of the artistic history of mankind. Poetry was designed to be sung and listened to, and visual elements simply did not enter in to the making of a poem. It was only after the advent of printing that the visually-orientated forms of poetry to which we are mainly accustomed in modern Western culture became dominant. Dylan's aural orientation is scarcely something new within a wider frame of reference. The complexity of the music to which many of his songs are set, however, *is* innovatory, and this often results in a reduced conduciveness to visual appreciation when the words are seen on the page. There are many things which the words (as written) do not have to do because the voice and the music are doing them. In printed poetry, because meaning is abstracted from the sound of the spoken word, total sense must be contained within what is written, whereas in Dylan's work much of the sense may be contributed by aspects of the music. Even such a quintessentially emotive phrase as "How does it feel? How does it feel?" can look cool, detached and unemotional in print. If it does not, or to the extent to which it does not, it is because we carry into our reading a knowledge of how it sounds when sung, perhaps in a variety of tones and moods. (Unless such a knowledge of how Dylan sounds could be assumed in the readers of this book, the writing of it would clearly be a fruitless exercise.) On the page the words may lose much of their emotional tonality, their dynamic properties, and become relatively inert. But (and this is the main theme of this chapter) this does not always happen, or not always to the same degree. Because Dylan's art is a mixed form, influenced by the traditions of Western poetry as well as by oral and aural determinants, it often has qualities which are closer to visual poetry than its primarily aural character might suggest.

Dylan will often use half-rhyme and assonance in ways which make them sound more or less like a full rhyme when sung: the structural patterns are intended for the ear and not for the eye. In 'When the Ship Comes In', for example, "laugh" rhymes with "path", "spoken" with "ocean", "roll" with "gold", "tribe" with "tide", "numbered" with "conquered". Similarly in 'Boots of Spanish Leather' we have "morning" corresponding to "landing", "ownin'" to "ocean" (twice), "golden" to "Barcelona". In 'Mr. Tambourine Man' "wanderin'" rhymes with "under it". Dylan is expert at bending sounds with his voice to turn them into rhymes. One of his favourite eccentric rhymes is that of "mirror" with words ending "-eer" or "-ear". It probably sounds much less strange to American ears than to British ones, but it must still look odd on the page:

> Louise, she's all right, she's just near
> She's delicate and seems like the mirror
> But she just makes it all to concise and too clear
> That Johanna's not here . . .

Dylan's pronunciation is roughly "meer'r", one and a half syllables. He uses the same rhyme internally in 'No Time to Think': "You glance through the mirror and there's eyes staring clear / At the back of your head as you drink"; and in 'Went to See the Gypsy' rhymes the word with "rear", "fear" and "here".

In these cases the aural principle enhances or fills out dubious rhymes; Dylan imposes heavy duty upon procedures which in written poetry would be reserved for subtler effects. But the opposite can happen too. More frequently, effects which would be too strong for the printed page are toned down, made into subtler instruments, by their musical context. The piled-up internal rhymes of 'All I Really Want to Do' provide a good example (though the phrase "internal rhyme" itself betrays a visual prejudice: it is often hard to say whether a Dylan rhyme is or is not internal, because the rhyming units correspond to musical phrases rather than printed lines):

> I don't want to straight-face you,
> Race or chase you, track or trace you,
> Or disgrace you or displace you,
> Or define you or confine you.

The swift rattle of rhyme and alliteration only makes its point fully within the musical scheme which carries it, where it retains no trace of the crudity which it may look to have in print. Similarly, this from 'Only a Pawn in Their Game' cannot be properly appreciated until heard:

> From the poverty shacks, he looks from the cracks
>   to the tracks,
> And the hoof beats pound in his brain.

The hurried, cramped delivery of the first line gives substance to a feeling of confinement, limitation and monotony; then the slow, drawn-out passion of the second gives us in contrast the sense of thrilling, intoxicated liberation. The incisive opening lines of 'Like a Rolling Stone', again, are too "heavy" for print:

> Once upon a time you dressed so fine
> You threw the bums a dime in your prime, didn't you?
> People'd call, say, "Beware doll, you're bound to fall"
> You thought they were all kiddin' you . . .

The machine-bug effects are here thrown into relief by the phrases "didn't you" and "kiddin' you", the emphasis on which is determined much more by the musical than by the verbal patterning.

There are whole songs whose rhythms differ essentially from those of a poem, and where the imagery is lusher, the effects brasher, the meaning thinner than would be acceptable in a poem that was not also a song; 'Chimes of Freedom' is a good example of such a work. 'Mr Tambourine Man' is more finely honed, the verbal patterning more careful, but the lyrics stand essentially as a "correspondence" to the music; they evoke through imagery a feeling which is evoked musically by the melody, but which has little intellectual content; in that sense this is musical poetry:

> Then take me disappearin' through the smoke rings of

my mind,
Down the foggy ruins of time, far past the frozen leaves,
The haunted, frightened trees, out to the windy beach,
Far from the twisted reach of crazy sorrow.
Yes, to dance beneath the diamond sky with one hand
    waving free,
Silhouetted by the sea, circled by the circus sands,
With all memory and fate driven deep beneath the waves,
Let me forget about today until tomorrow.

Though the imagery is visual in character it is impressed upon us, forced upon our attention primarily through the sound effects, the very strong rhyming, assonance and alliteration, and the patterns which these form relate to the structure of the music and not to any design based upon a visual principle. We respond to this poetry for its evocative qualities, as they fall musically upon our ear, and the eye is not on the scene to rest upon a phrase like "circus sands", ask just what it pictures, and conclude that it is there mainly to provide an assonance with the preceding "circled".

When setting his songs out on the page Dylan does nevertheless pay attention to the needs of the eye in making sense of the words. Sometimes he will transfer a phrase from its true position in the aural pattern so as to make a sense unit of a line. This happens several times in 'It's Alright, Ma', as for example in the second verse:

> Pointed threats, they bluff with scorn
> Suicide remarks are torn
> From the fool's gold mouthpiece
> The hollow horn plays wasted words . . .

As sung, "The hollow horn" forms a rhythmic continuum with the preceding line, which tends to break up the meaning; printed like this, it is both easier to follow the sense and to savour the image of "the fool's gold mouthpiece" which otherwise tends to be submerged in the general flood of words. (The end rhyme of "horn" with "torn" is naturally lost to the eye, but it is strong enough anyway for this not to matter.)

It does sometimes happen like this, that the music and words interact in such a way as to make it difficult to follow the sense. This does not often matter much in the earlier Dylan, where a great deal of the excitement of the lyrics lies in the sudden stab of reality, often of psychological recognition, out of the prolixity and obscurity of the images – such moments are usually carefully constructed so as to allow the maximum impact. In the later work, however, where the poetry is more conscious and defined, such "clashes of interest" can operate, as we shall see, to the disadvantage of the latter. There are some songs which are almost poems set to music, in which the language is dense and complex enough to make listening by itself insufficient for full appreciation; we need to supplement our aural acquaintance by familiarity with the text, and thus armed return to the music. In some of the narrative songs, too, notably 'Black Diamond Bay', the action is almost too swift and involved to be followed by the ear.

One of the most exacting tasks in the reconciling of the demands of the reading eye with aural patterning, when transferring the lyrics to the printed page, must have been presented by 'Visions of Johanna', and it is very effectively surmounted in the *Writings and Drawings* text. This great song reads very well as a poem, yet its concertina-like structure, based on expandable musical units, appears at first glance to militate against the possibility. The underlying rhyme scheme is shown straightforwardly by the first verse: AAA BBBB CC. This scheme is in fact strictly adhered to throughout (except that, as we saw in Chapter Two, the final stanza expands to allow for three extra B lines), but it is concealed in all the later verses by expansion *within* the basic lines, achieved through miracles of inspired phrasing. In setting out the lines for the page Dylan has worked on a principle of making each line a sense unit, so that there may or may not be extra lines which accommodate expansions of the musical phrases; the basic lines may be telescoped together if the sense calls for it, or broken up even where there is no expansion. All these processes can be seen in the third stanza: it has the same number of printed lines as the paradigmatic first, but they are quite differently arranged, even though the underlying rhyme scheme is maintained for the ear:

Now little boy lost, he takes himself so seriously
He brags of his misery, he likes to live dangerously
And when bringing her name up
He speaks of a farewell kiss to me
He's sure got a lotta gall to be so useless and all
Muttering small talk at the wall while I'm in the hall
How can I explain?
Oh, it's so hard to get on
And these visions of Johanna, they kept me up past the dawn.

What has happened here is that the third A line has expanded to provide lines three and four, the four B lines have been contracted to two (with extra internal rhyming in the second), and the first C line has been split into lines seven and eight of the printed verse. This arrangement answers to the sense of the words as apprehended by the eye, without any disturbance of the aural pattern, that being strong enough to take care of itself. Dylan's most prodigious feat of phrasing and breath control is however reserved for the final verse, whose three basic A lines are set out like this:

> The peddler now speaks to the countess who's pretending
>   to care for him
> Sayin', "Name me someone who's not a parasite and I'll go
>   out and say a prayer for him"
> But like Louise always says
> "Ya can't look at much, can ya man?"
> As she, herself, prepares for him . . .

It can be seen that the sense unit principle operates again here, so that the first two rhyming lines are not split up in spite of their great length, while the phenomenally long third divides into three. And while on the subject of phrasing, it is worth just looking, with a memory of how it is sung, at an amazing pair of lines from another *Blonde on Blonde* song, 'Absolutely Sweet Marie':

> Well, anybody can be like me, obviously,
> But then, now again, not too many can be like you,
>   fortunately.

This aspect of Dylan's artistry probably reaches its peak on *Blonde on Blonde*.

The experience of writing *John Wesley Harding* in a more conscious, less spontaneous and overflowing way than the albums which came before it probably had a permanent effect on Dylan's approach to composing his songs. In the records which immediately follow it the structure of the lyrics is simple in the main; they cannot be looked at as if they were in any sense poems. When Dylan emerges from his country period with *Planet Waves*, into renewed complexity of theme and richness of language, the lyrics are tauter, more "defined" in his own phrase,[6] controlled by a more disciplined simplicity. Often, the stress seems when we are listening to be mainly on the music: the words do not draw attention to themselves, tending to sound like an underlining of the musical message, a "punctuation" of the sound, to borrow Dylan's terminology once again.[7] Paradoxically, though, they sometimes stand on their own feet on the page much better than many earlier songs whose lyrics are imposed on our attention more successfully. This is true, I think, of 'Tough Mama':

> Dark Beauty
> Won't you move it on over and make some room
> It's my duty
> To bring you down to the field where the flowers bloom
> Ashes in the furnace

Dust on the rise
You came through it all the way
Flyin' through the skies
Dark Beauty
With that long night's journey in your eyes

This number, which I take to be a hymn to Dylan's returning Muse, is marked by a sharply realised field of imagery and a more continuous thread of sense than can easily be picked up by the half-attentive ear. In 'Never Say Goodbye', also, we are so aware of the sound-poem which is the music that concentration tends to focus on a number of separate phrases and pictures and we fail to take in the connected lyric sense which is actually there.

Blood on the Tracks and *Desire*, on the other hand, achieve a very satisfactory integration of the musical and verbal components and there are few instances of one working against the other, though as noticed earlier the events of the more complicated narratives can be hard to follow at early hearings. Some versions of 'Shelter from the Storm' do however yield an example of how lazy phrasing can break up sense:

> In a world of steel-eyed death and men
> Who are fighting to be warm / born . . .

In the recorded concert treatments (less so in the original) Dylan makes little effort to connect "and men" with the following clause with which it belongs, so that it sounds as if "steel-eyed" qualifies "men" as well as "death". It is hard to imagine the Dylan of *Blonde on Blonde* failing to find a solution to this problem; and in fact he carries off beautifully a comparable moment in 'Simple Twist of Fate':

> He felt the heat of the night
> Hit him like a freight train
> Moving with a simple twist of fate.

"Train" is here trapped, as it were, between two lines, "freight" really providing an end-rhyme with "fate", but Dylan experiences no difficulty in coping with it. The structure of 'Hurricane' makes good use of phrases similarly caught in the middle: in most verses the penultimate line contains two rhymes, one of which refers backwards to the preceding line and the other forwards to the following. In verse seven an extra internal rhyme is thrown in for good measure:

> ". . . We want to put his ass in stir
> We want to pin this triple murder on him
> He ain't no Gentleman Jim"

131

The two syllables of "murder" each command a stress equal to that on "him".

It is on *Street-Legal* that tensions between music and poetry are most in evidence, and these tensions inflict some damage upon our appreciation of certain of the songs as integrated wholes. This is noticeable because the lyrics are of a very high quality, and though the music too is remarkable it does not always display the words to the best advantage. In two of the most impressive songs on the album, *Señor* and 'Where Are You Tonight?', the balance succeeds, with striking poetry and magnificent music working together and defining each other; but in two others, 'Changing of the Guards' and 'No Time to Think,' they sometimes seem to act at cross-purposes. The latter is a fine song, reminiscent of some of the classics of 1965–66 in its interspersing of arresting and exotic, if sometimes obscure imagery with swift flashes of insight, and like them too it is notable for the intensity of its portrayal of the disaffected individual at war with society and self. Unfortunately Dylan's performance is uncharacteristically sloppy, marred by poor diction and careless phrasing, and the unsatisfactory sound of the record – at once harsh and muffled, especially on Side One – adds to the resultant confusion. He has admitted[8] that the record was made in a hurry, and it shows. Some of the problems however spring not essentially from the performance but from the relation between verbal and musical structure. The first clear example occurs in verse three:

> I've seen all these decoys through a set of deep turquoise eyes
> And I feel so depressed.

The rhyme of "turquoise" with "decoys" ends a musical phrase; "eyes" belongs, in all ways except that of semantic meaning, with the line that follows. Dylan sings the words in accordance with the strict dictates of the melodic line, and indeed his scope for doing anything else is very limited. The result is to break "turquoise" and "eyes" completely apart, and the effect is not at all pleasing. On the other hand the way the lines are set out on the page is not satisfactory either, for the placing of "eyes" in the earlier line interferes with the integrated expectations of eye and ear: the rule of one idea to a line is observed at the expense of rhythm. Nor is this principle necessary here: the reader of poetry is perfectly accustomed to run-ons between lines. Exactly the same thing occurs in the eighth verse: "The bridge that you travel on goes to the Babylon girl / With the rose in her hair". The device works properly only in the splendid final verse:

> Bullets can harm you and death can disarm you,
> But no, you will not be deceived.

Stripped of all virtue as you crawl through the dirt,
You can give but you cannot receive.

The rhythmic movement here is not all disturbed by the split rhyme
in lines three and four. Although "dirt" and "You" combine to
rhyme with "virtue", "You" belongs with what follows it both
semantically and in terms of its position in the melodic line. In this
case, too, the *separation* of the two words on the page (again in
accordance with meaning) avoids the kind of assault on the senses
which Byron is liable to perpetrate in his more eccentric moments:

> The General Boone, backwoodsman of Kentucky,
> Was happiest among mortals anywhere!
> For killing nothing but a bear or buck, he
> Enjoyed the lonely, vigorous, harmless days
> Of his old age in wilds of deepest maze.

In 'No Time to Think' Dylan has experienced a certain difficulty
in reconciling complicated lyrical and musical patterns, and this has
resulted in a few localised clumsinesses. In 'Changing of the Guards'
the problem is more general and harder to pinpoint. The song's
imagery, in the first place, is exceedingly dense; it cannot really be
taken in by the ear alone. The story (for there is one) is broken,
dreamlike and elusive; the album's poor production, already
referred to, makes individual words hard to identify. On top of all
this, the musical pattern tends, in several verses, to be at odds with
the lyric structure and to break it up. This can perhaps be seen most
clearly in verse six. The words read so well that we may wonder
whether the song was not conceived as a poem and then set to
music, or at least whether each component did not have a separate
evolution.

> The palace of mirrors
> Where dog soldiers are reflected;
> The endless road and the wailing of chimes;
> The empty rooms where her memory is protected
> Where the angels' voices whisper to the souls of
>   previous times.

The conflict between words and music can only be illustrated by
setting the lyrics out in a different way, reflecting as closely as possible the phrasing with which they are sung. The repetitions in
brackets represent the echoes contributed by the back-up singers,
which form an integral part of the pattern:

> The palace of mirrors (palace of mirrors)
> Where dog soldiers are reflected; the endless road

(endless road)
And the wailing of chimes; the empty rooms
(empty rooms)
Where her memory is protected;
Where the angels' voices whisper
To the souls of previous times.

The insecurity of the relation between rhythm and sense is easily observable here: words which belong with each other are forced apart, and others which should have a distance between them are yoked together by the dominance of the musical form. The problem relates, it must be said, to the ambition of what is being attempted. It is very hard to fit such dense, complex and difficult poetry to a melody and make it work smoothly in a succession of verses with widely differing grammatical structures. Rather than scrutinising the instances in which it is not entirely brought off we should perhaps rather be wondering at those in which the feat is successfully accomplished, as it notably is in the last two verses of the song (quoted in full in Chapter Four). The caesuras here fall in such a way that meaning and music are in harmony throughout, and the poetic form is enhanced by the musical design.

The main point to be made about these *Street-Legal* songs in the present context, however, is how well some of them – and especially, perhaps, 'Changing of the Guards' and 'Where Are You Tonight?' – do stand up on the page. Unlike many earlier pieces which certainly work better *as songs*, they do not have that limp, flat look in print for which we have to compensate out of our memory of the sound. This suggests strongly that if the time were ever to come when Dylan was unable to sing, he could develop into a poet of major stature in the traditional visually-orientated mode. There is no reason to suppose at the time of writing, though, that such is the direction in which he is likely to move. On *Slow Train Coming* he is very much writing songs again, rather than musical poems, and showing no signs of any decline in his talents in that form. It is a very strong record both musically and lyrically, and in its boldness and conceptual clarity leaves behind the dilemmas we have been discussing. This, in its turn, need not indicate that he will not return to making songs out of a richer and more complicated poetry. The most constant feature of Dylan's development is that it has never been straightforwardly linear: a particular tendency may become dominant for a time and be traceable through a number of albums, but on each one he is attempting something different, something that belongs to it alone. Like Baudelaire, he has made it his consistent artistic endeavour "in the depths of the Unknown to find the *new*!"

Chapter Six:

Dodging Lions

> Oh, the hours I've spent inside the Coliseum,
> Dodging lions and wastin' time.
> Oh, those mighty kings of the jungle, I could scarcely stand
> to see 'em,
> Yes, it sure has been a long, hard climb.

The history of Dylan's relations with the media, and to some extent with his public, has the marks of a prolonged gladiatorial contest; long before he was a Christian he seems to have had the sense of being thrown to the lions. He has survived, and repeatedly come out on top, precisely by dodging, by taking the measure of the opposition, anticipating which way they will jump next, and keeping always one step ahead. Throughout his career he has lived on his wits and thought on his feet. In the running battle with the reporters who want to turn him into "the boy nex' door" and the fans who seek in him an idealised mirror image of themselves, Dylan has defended himself by making some startling changes of direction and adopting a succession of sharply divergent images and personas. Being true to himself has involved consciously negating other people's conceptions of what he is or ought to be. The problem is concisely stated in 'Maggie's Farm':

> Well, I try my best
> To be just like I am,
> But everybody wants you
> To be just like them.
> They say sing while you slave and I just get bored.
> I ain't gonna work on Maggie's Farm no more.

It need not be doubted that there is an element of cock-snooking in the refusal: Dylan gets a kick out of shocking people and upsetting their expectations. Deeper than that, though, is the need to assert that he does not belong to anyone, that his life and his art are his own and his future development is not a matter for comfortable pre-diction. In the butter sculptor's letter in *Tarantula* (quoted from at the beginning of this book), the artist tells the critic: ". . . i must go

135

now – i have this new hunk of margarine waiting in the bathtub – yes i said MARGARINE & next week i might just decide to use cream cheese – "[1] These words register the strain that comes from being constantly a focus of eager expectations. They shed light on, though they do not "explain", a good deal in Dylan's development.

The changing forms of Dylan's self-image have however another, more positive function: they help to define him to himself, and thus make possible the successful projections of that self in art. Without wishing to venture into psychology, I have the impression that he has never been too sure of who he is outside his art. At the beginning of his career the fictions which he put about concerning his upbringing and experience threatened to get out of control – they have a memorial in the jacket notes to his first album which now reads rather touchingly. The "simple country boy" persona which he made use of in those early days was the most useful and fruitful of this set of fictions, for it afforded him a point of entry into a vital range of musical attitudes and conventions and left permanent marks on his use of language. But it *was* a fiction: in no sense was Dylan ever a simple country boy, in background, intention or cast of mind. The value of the convention lay in providing him with a framework within which he could make sense of his own feelings, and into which he could project them. Like subsequent images, it didn't at first appear to be what was wanted. 'Talking New York' records how when Dylan got on the stage of a coffee house in Greenwich Village he was given his marching orders: "You sound like a hillbilly; / We want folk singers here." Things were not slow to change.

Much breath has been wasted in discussing whether or not Dylan was sincere in becoming a folk singer and writer of political songs; many felt at the time of his move to electric rock (and he himself said much which encouraged the idea) that his adoption of these roles had been essentially cynical, aimed at securing the most readily available passport to fame. The fact is, of course, that all human motives – including those of artists – are mixed. Artists, like other people, can share in feelings of the day and participate in contemporary trends and movements; if they did not do so, they would lose much of their representative quality. Like others, too, they can change, move forward on the wave of a new impulse when an old one is exhausted; if they did not do that they could not develop. In New York in 1961–64 it would have been impossible for someone in Dylan's situation to have remained uninfluenced by what was going on all around him. More artists than Dylan found themselves artistically in that ferment: there are some who hold that Phil Ochs, for example, wrote better protest songs. That others did not move on as Dylan did may tell us less about the comparative depth of their sincerity than about the relative range and possibilities of their talents. To continue to work in a certain form, or to stop doing so, has nothing to do with artistic sincerity. To test that, we must look to the content of the work: if it speaks truly to us we may assume that it does not proceed from a false emotion. Dylan's protest songs spoke truly to many thousands of people in the early sixties, and many of them have stood the test of time.

That is not to deny that when Dylan did start working with an electric band it was essentially a homecoming. He has said that it was an Odetta record which turned him on to folk singing around 1958: "Right then and there, I went out and traded my electric guitar and amplifier for an acoustical guitar, a flat-top Gibson."[2] Later "a whole new world" was opened up for him by Woody Guthrie. But of the switch back to electric rock he commented: "Well, it had to get there. It had to go that way for me. Because that's where I started and eventually it just got back to that."[3] It was impossible for him to go on being "the lone folkie" because he heard his songs as "part of the music, the musical background."

It is noteworthy that his finest periods, which I take to be the mid sixties and the mid seventies, have been those in which he has least used the support of limiting concepts of himself, in which he has found ways to be himself, and express that artistically, without the intermediacy of any confining persona. The rock flowering of the mid sixties, though it was as much an articulation of a contemporary public feeling as was the protest movement, was more suited to the pursuit of artistic individualism. Dylan was one of its chief architects and its greatest exponent; yet by the time it was at its apogee he had moved on. *John Wesley Harding*, that stark, understated and introspective album, was entirely unexpected and, to contemporaries, oddly in contrast with such lavish productions as the Rolling Stones' *Beggar's Banquet* and the Beatles' *Sergeant Pepper*.[4] It marked the transition to the long dalliance with country music which took in Dylan's next three albums and left his following uncertain as to whether he would ever re-emerge. If he did lose control of the accompanying persona he succeeded in regaining it again; but later on he was aware that at this period he had been going against his own nature: "I was trying to grasp something that would lead me on to where I thought I should be, and it didn't go nowhere – it just went down, down, down. I couldn't be anybody but myself, and at that point I didn't know it or want to know it."[5] This relates to one of the truths which he has said he was trying to express in *Renaldo and Clara*, truths which came from accumulated experience and "a knowledge that I aquired on the road"; "One is that if you try to be anyone but yourself, you will fail; if you are not true to your own heart, you will fail. Then again, there's no success like failure."[6] That qualification, and the truth which *it* expresses, are typical of Dylan's scrupulous faithfulness to experience.

His development in the seventies has tended to show that Jon Landau was right when he claimed that Dylan's capacity to grow "is too great to sustain any particular myth for too long, or for him to lose control of it."[7] With the conversion to Christianity, though, this thesis seems set to be tested once more. As in the past, Dylan is not moving in isolation: Dave Marsh has pointed out that "*Slow Train Coming* is linked with several other recent albums in a trend towards overtly spiritual rock & roll."[8] (He cites Robert Fripp's *Exposure*, Arlo Guthrie's *Outlasting the Blues*, and Van Morrison's *Into the Mystic*.) The album's revival of apocalypticism, again, coincided with a fresh mood of anxiety in Western culture and anticipated a sudden worsening in international relations which is propagating a renewed fear of nuclear war. It would not be surprising if the next year or two were to witness an upsurge of apocalyptic fears and perhaps of a corresponding religious renewal. Whatever happens to Dylan next, it will certainly not be unrelated to what is happening to the rest of mankind.

A consciousness of the final irrelevance of any public role which might be thrust upon the artist has always been one of the features of Dylan's realism and sense of proportion. Asked by *Playboy* in 1966 whether he wouldn't like "to help the young people who dig you from turning into what some of their parents have become?" he rejoined: "Well, I must say that I really don't know their parents . . . I'm not about to save anybody from fate, which I know nothing about. 'Parents' is not the key word here. The key word is destiny. I can't save them from that."[9] The same interview sees him rebutting again and again, with style and quick intelligence, the efforts of the interviewer to extract from him some acceptable concession to comfortable liberal pieties. His attitude to these questions of the artist's public involvement has remained consistent: his position has always been to resist the connection between any social or political *content* in his songs and a simplistic view of their social *function*. Thus his unexpected release of a protest song in 1971 – the single 'George Jackson' – is not contradicted by his reiteration, in 'Wedding Song' from the *Planet Waves* album, that

> It's never been my duty
> To remake the world at large
> Nor is it my intention
> To sound a battle charge . . .

It is clear from the tone of all his responses on these subjects that his antagonism is not really to the concept of artistic responsibility but to that of the artist's *accountability*. In an interview with Michael

March in 1969 he commented, "I say what I have to, man. The artist is the most political figure in society because he stands outside. *John Wesley Harding* is religious and political – besides, they're both the same thing."[10]

Ellen Willis, as we saw in Chapter One, called Dylan a "fifth-columnist from the past"; and nowhere is his fifth-column quality more apparent than in his championing of privacy in the face of the attempts of the media to turn him into public property. *Playboy*, announcing their 1978 interview with him, referred to him as "the reclusive one". In reality, he has never been reluctant to answer intelligent or even just sensible questions with the respect which they deserve; but in the early years such questions were seldom asked him. The interviews of the late seventies, in their relative openness and their useful stress upon his career and his artistic attitudes, provide a marked contrast with those of the nineteen-sixties, in many of which Dylan was fighting a guerrilla campaign against impertinence and dim wits. The new mellowness reflects not so much any change in Dylan's attitude towards the press as one in the press's attitude towards him, a change forced on it by the success of his tactics. The focus of attention has switched from his private life, his opinions and his attitudes, to what he is doing in his art, and that Dylan has shown himself prepared to talk about freely.

There is no doubt that it is the very openness with which he has used his private experience and his personal feelings in his songs which has encouraged inappropriate kinds of interest in his life. Few people are prepared to recognise the autonomy of art which uses the personal to say something universal; which may arise from preoccupations which are private but functions at a level which is impersonal and objective. The very degree of self-exposure which Dylan permits himself in art must make his personal privacy more important to him. So he hits out, in the 'Outlined Epitaph' which deals with magazine reporters, at those who seek

> t' bust me down
> an' "expose" me
> in their own terms
> givin' blind advice
> t' unknown eyes
> who have no way of knowin'
> that I "expose" myself
> every time I step out
> on the stage . . .

Resentment at this treatment has not lessened with the years: in 1978 he takes up the same theme with *Rolling Stone*. Referring to critics of *Street-Legal* and *Renaldo and Clara* he says, "Look, just one time I'd like to see any one of those assholes try and do what I do. Just once let one of them write a song to show how they feel and sing it in front of ten, let alone 10,000 or 100,000 people. I'd like to see them just try that one time."[11]

Nowhere in Dylan's work does the creative tension between the private life and its public exploitation raise so many questions as in his film *Renaldo and Clara*, made mostly during the Rolling Thunder Review tour of 1975–76 and released early in 1978. In spite of winning a prize at the Cannes Film Festival, the movie was torn to pieces by most of the critics, and mostly on the grounds of self-indulgence, pretentiousness and egotism on the part of its maker. This was perhaps the inevitable fate of a film which seemed to present, interspersed with marvellous concert footage from the tour and much documentary, cinema-verité material, a cartoon-like projection of events in Dylan's life in which principal parts were taken by himself, his wife and Joan Baez. In these fictional parts of the film Dylan plays the part of a certain Renaldo and Sara Dylan that of his woman Clara, while Ronnie Hawkins, the Canadian rock star – someone about as physically unlike Dylan as it is possible to imagine – goes by the name of "Bob Dylan". Elsewhere, Dylan is seen as himself, though except when he is singing his role is distinguished chiefly by its silence and passivity.

Dylan has spoken at some length on what he feels his film to be about.[12] Man, he said, is alienated from himself and in order to be reborn has to "go outside himself". Renaldo is seeking to hide from "the demon within", but at length sees that this demon is a "mirrored reflection" of himself. Through the film Dylan attempts to express certain truths which have come to him with experience, such as that being untrue to oneself brings inevitable failure; being untrue to oneself is equatable with a kind of death. The audience "shouldn't even think they know anyone in this film" – it is essentially fictional. There is no "real" Bob Dylan in the movie: "His voice is there, his songs are used, but Bob is not in the movie. It would be silly. Did you ever see a Picasso painting with Picasso in the picture? You only see his work." The reason the name Bob Dylan is used is "In order to legitimize this film. We confronted it head on: The persona of Bob Dylan is in the movie so we could get rid of it. There should no longer be any mystery as to who or what he is – he's there, speaking in all kinds of tongues, and there's even someone else claiming to be him, so he's covered." The film, Dylan claims, is open and accessible; "If it doesn't move you then it's a grand, grand failure." He reacts somewhat equivocally to the suggestion that "the movie is really intended to take on the gossip about you head on": he agrees that there is some truth in that, but resists the idea that the question is very important. "This movie is taking experience and turning it into something else," he finishes the discussion by saying. "It's not a gossipy movie."

All this suggests that the real purpose of the film is to enact a parable about the artist's identity. It is one more round in Dylan's long struggle to keep separate his self and the art which proceeds from it. The more abstract intentions which he talks of are not very clearly articulated: what does come across with the most vivid immediacy is the contrast between on the one hand both the persona of Renaldo *and* the Dylan who appears in the documentary scenes, and on the other the man on the stage who sings the songs. In the four hours of the uncut version we can count on our fingers the number of times Dylan speaks, and when he does so it is seldom more than a few mumbled words. Repeatedly there are scenes in which people talk at him and he listens, in passive receptivity; in one scene in a bar a man jabbers away for minutes while Dylan mostly contemplates his glass, registering scarcely any feeling or reaction. Yet he controls everything that happens. Renaldo, his creature, also controls situations through his very passivity. He seems to be played upon, tugged emotionally from Clara by the Woman in White (played by Joan Baez) and then tugged, physically, back again; he appears like a little child, smothered and overwhelmed by the attentions of his rival lovers, yet in the end it is they who are manipulated by him, who ask him questions which he will not answer, who seek from him what he withholds. Clara may have his body, but neither of them has his soul. The audience, too, does not get what it seeks (or what the director suspects it of seeking). The film says nothing about Dylan the man; one can go further and suggest that its substance, finally, consists in the refusal to say anything about Dylan the man. Far from confronting the "gossip" head on, it merely tantalises the curiosity of the audience with a cartoon version of what they already know. Yet the fictional scenes are often related, by juxtaposition, to the songs which Dylan performs; and it is here that the obverse side of his argument is enacted. Do you want to know the truth? he asks. Very well, *here* is the truth – in my songs. Here, and nowhere else, is where I expose myself.

And expose himself he does. Every cut from fictional scene to stage performance is a switch from a situation in which Dylan is a cipher, an insubstantial symbol, to one in which he is a vibrant, responsive and expressive being, life issuing from him in overflowing superabundance. We see "close shots of Dylan in white face spitting and barking out twenty-two of his classics with demonic power – songs we know in a way we've never known them before";[13] and the mystery of where all this comes from remains undisturbed. Picasso is not in the painting – we see only his work. Dylan is physically present when he sings, of course, but he is present as *part* of the work, in that his songs do not exist without him: "The man behind the myth" doesn't get a look-in. Asked about the danger that "your own myths will subvert what you say is the purpose of the movie", he replies: "Don't forget – I'm not a myth to myself. Only to others. If others didn't create that myth of Bob Dylan, there would be no myth of Bob Dylan in the movie." It is as if he were saying, It is only the fact that I write and perform songs that makes me different from anyone else. That being so, it is my songs that your attention should be directed to, not myself. The point is underlined in a scene in which virtue departs from him when he stops singing. He walks off the stage and straight to a back room where he flops on the floor, drained and empty, and remains lying there, the camera circling about his prone form, while "life outside goes on all around [him]".

The silent, nebulous Dylan of *Renaldo and Clara*, it must be emphasised, no more reflects the "real" one than does any other persona he adopts. It is scarcely accidental that when he makes his first appearance in the movie, singing 'When I Paint my Masterpiece' as the credits roll, he is wearing a mask; and in subsequent performances his face is concealed by dead-white make-up. His individual personality is thus symbolically blotted out while he sings – he is the mouthpiece of a higher power. As he has said, "When you're playing music and it's going well, you do lose your identity, you become totally subservient to the music you're doing in your very being... But later on, backstage, you have a different point of view."[14] But this everyday personality is eternally elusive: it is private, and as he has no intention of exhibiting it, in its place his public construct the myth. While abjuring any responsibility for "the myth of Bob Dylan", and making no concessions to it, Dylan is careful not to destroy it, for he is shrewd enough to be aware of its value to him; instead, he conscientiously and systematically evades it. At one of its levels, *Renaldo and Clara* is his most ambitious exercise yet in lion-dodging.

The one way in which Dylan maintains a continuing and developing relationship with his public is through his songs, especially perhaps those that they know well. As he sings his old songs in new ways he redefines his feelings, tells his audience how he has changed and is changing, and reflects the changes which have overtaken them. There are things that can be said more succinctly through the recreation of the old than through the creation of the new, and this element of creative renovation is an important one in Dylan's art. As I argued early on in this study, he is one of the first major artists to be emancipated from the visually-determined sense of permanence and unalterability in the work of art. His songs are not fixed for all time in the forms in which he first recorded them; but it took critics a while to get used to the extent of the remakings he was ready to impose on them, for the assumption of total freedom which underlies this activity implies the principles of a new aesthetic.

Dylan alters his songs in many different ways. Sometimes he will rewrite the words, either in part or in whole: this has happened to 'Lay Lady Lay', about which he "always had a feeling there was more to the song" than came out in the original;[15] to 'Going, Going, Gone', which has become a song about leaving a lover instead of one about changing a life; and, as we have seen, to 'Simple Twist of Fate'. A very slight verbal change can on occasions underline a general transformation of mood, as in the *Budokan* version of 'The Times They Are A-Changin'' where we have "the loser now might be later to win" instead of "will" – a change which mirrors Dylan's journey from innocence to experience in the fifteen years since he wrote the song. That gesture towards making the alteration of viewpoint explicit contributes much to the stature of the treatment – the element of simplistic optimism is toned down and implicitly criticised, so that the more enduring aspects, benefiting from Dylan's continuing faith in them, acquire greater depth and new resonances of meaning; the song now speaks to a sadder and more disillusioned generation.

Sometimes it is the music which has changed. The versions of the 1974 tour, preserved in *Before the Flood*, revealed the potentialities of 'All Along the Watchtower' as a hard rock number; gave us a raging, full-blooded 'It's Alright, Ma', far removed from the tight, restrained intensity of the acoustic rendering; breathed new life into 'Blowin' in the Wind', showing it to be a much more lasting and resilient song than most of us had supposed; informed 'Just Like a Woman' with driving passion. 'I Threw It All Away', a bland, almost casual country number on *Nashville Skyline*, burns as something felt and experienced on *Hard Rain*; 'One Too Many Mornings', as well as acquiring an extra verse, becomes an expression of a quite different emotional attitude. And for an example of how changes of rhythm, tempo and melody can alter the "feel" of what a song is saying without any modifications to the words, we have the *Budokan* variation of 'Oh, Sister'.

Dylan has said that in order for a song to endure years after the occasion that called it forth "there's got to be something to it that is real – not just for the moment."[16] He admits that he has written many songs that, for him, do not stand the test of time in that way. It is strange, though, that he never returns to some of his greatest songs – 'Desolation Row', for example, or 'Visions of Johanna'. Perhaps these are creations whose character is more fixed and absolute, which are too defined to allow for reworking; or perhaps they are just too long. 'Like a Rolling Stone', on the other hand, is a masterpiece to which Dylan has again and again brought the core of himself, the essence of how he feels. To listen to the different ways he has sung it is like running an eye over his spiritual history. To confine ourselves to officially released versions – the original, made at the zenith of his early fame, breathes an almost dismissive confidence, a certainty of his own rightness. The Isle of Wight rendition, included on *Self Portrait*, negates its own meaning: in its almost affected innocuousness, its weak amiability, it speaks for a Dylan trying to conceal from himself his own nature, to be someone other than himself. On *Before the Flood*, in total contrast, the song is a celebration of rediscovered power; the spirit is one of exultant, vindictive bitterness, the message driven home with dramatic thrust. The *Budokan* 'Rolling Stone', though, is the most surprising and revealing of all: it is sad. Who would have imagined that this could become a *sympathetic* song? The Dylan of 1978 is mature, understanding and large-spirited – he is not even saying "I told you so". This version seems to carry all its predecessors within it – it includes them as implicit points of reference, summates and transcends them. The sweep and power of the music are unequalled; never have the "dynamics of the rhythm", which Dylan identifies as the key to the song, been so movingly explored.

This process of renewal is vital because it keeps his work in a dynamic relation to his changing and expanding audience. The songs live in a slightly different way, say something subtly fresh, to each new rank of Dylan followers, as well as reflecting the effects of time on his old ones. One sometimes hears it said that he still largely depends for his support on those who grew up with his music in the sixties, but this is palpably untrue. I am two months younger than Dylan, and when I heard him in concert in Denver, Colorado in November 1978 I was certainly among the very oldest of the fourteen- or fifteen-thousand strong audience: most were in their early twenties, many still in their teens. At the same time, this young audience clearly has an intimate acquaintance with the whole range of his work, not merely his most recent albums: the classics of the sixties still command tremendous loyalty and enthusiasm, and much of the excitement lies in wondering how they will be treated. It is therefore disturbing to read reports, recent at the time of writing, of Dylan in a series of concerts on the American west coast in the winter of 1979–80 making what one reporter called the "brash gesture" of refusing to sing anything earlier than *Slow Train Coming*.[17] To turn his back on his past in this way seems a gratuitous act of will which suggests uncertainty rather than real confidence, and would, if it persists, make a poor testimonial indeed for his present standpoint. Henry Miller, whom Dylan has described as "the greatest American writer",[18] once wrote, "Tomorrow is no hazardous affair, a day like any other: tomorrow is the result of many yesterdays and comes with a potent, cumulative effect. I am tomorrow what I chose to be yesterday and the day before. It is not possible that tomorrow I may negate and nullify everything that led me to this present moment."[19]

For all that Dylan has often been at odds with those who have most admired him, for all that he has had to dodge the snares of the media and overturn the expectations of a public some of whom would like to recreate him in their own image, his relationship with those to whom his art speaks must, by the very nature of art, be a collaborative one: his songs live fully only as they are received. An artist's development, besides, is a continuum: belief in what one is doing in the present comes only out of proved experience of what is sound, true and real. Dylan has always said that he *believes* in his old songs, or the most enduring of them: "A lot of them *do* work. With those, there's some truth about every one of them. And I don't think I'd be singing if I weren't writing, you know ... Oh, yes. I've given new life to a lot of them. Because I believe in them, basically. You know, I believe in them."[20] And again, "They *are* real, and that's why I keep doing them."[21] Dylan has a naturally mercurial temperament, but some things should not change. To deny the validity of his artistic past is to undermine the value of his present, to pull its foundations from under it, to tear out its roots. To do that in order to make any kind of point to anyone would be to embrace unreality, to "let death creep in and take over a part of your life that should be alive." And to quote Dylan one final time, "The world is full of nonsupporters and backbiters – people who chew on wet rags. But it's also filled with people who love you."[22]

Postscript:

Saved

Saved, issued after the completion of the main body of this study, requires of the Dylan fan a far greater effort of reorientation and adaptation than its predecessor *Slow Train Coming*. The earlier album, once the initial shock of its content had been absorbed, was quick to reveal itself as an expression of the authentic Dylan voice, as even those most antagonistic to its message were constrained to admit. The recognition of that authentic voice in the new record is, except at isolated moments, *harder*. Yet the album's impetus, it seems to me, arises out of the sincerest of the impulses which underlie *Slow Train Coming*: the effort towards humility and self-effacement. It is an inescapable paradox, perhaps, that the degree to which it succeeds at an artistic level is commensurate with that of its failure to achieve complete self-abnegation.

The attempt begins with the cover and the title. It cannot be an accident that Dylan's two Christian albums are nearly alone in dispensing with his image on the outer cover. The design in this case – in decided contrast to the restraint and good taste which marked the presentation of *Slow Train Coming* – is almost defiantly vulgar, while the title is a starkly self-conscious cliché. The key to Dylan's motivation here must lie in the "higher calling" referred to in 'Pressing On'. This calling to the service of Christ is presumably being thought of as higher than his earlier calling to the service of art: the ends of art are being subordinated to, rather than made to work for, the spiritual purpose. It is not a position which it is useful to argue about – the matter is one of personal feeling, though it does occur to me that a possible answer to the question "What can I do for you?", which Dylan addresses to Jesus, might be: "Show that being a Christian is not incompatible with remaining a great artist." But that answer may not allow for the apparent need for self-sacrifice which Dylan is presently demonstrating. "Have I surrendered to the will of God / Or am I still acting like the boss?" he asks in 'Are You Ready?'; while we remember his recurrent urge to disappoint popular expectations when he sings of Jesus in 'In the Garden':

SAVED

The multitude wanted to make Him king,
Put a crown upon His head,
Why did He slip away
To a quiet place instead?

It is almost as if Dylan has chosen artistic self-abnegation as his personal Calvary.

A frequently encountered response to these new songs, but one which misses an important point, is that the music is competently professional and often rather stirring, but the lyrics banal and simplistic. The forms are certainly far more traditional than those of *Slow Train Coming*. Both music and words are closer to the norms of spiritual and gospel styles, in which it is the manner of singing that counts, to a degree which makes the quality of the lyrics almost irrelevant; and precisely in this we can see Dylan's effort to suppress some measure of his individuality, or at least to shift the emphasis to something less *obviously* individual, i.e. a purely vocal expressiveness. In his previous development, besides, there was often a noticeable equation between on the one hand the quest for sincerity and, on the other, an almost naive simplicity of utterance. We can say that at times when he has been trying to do what he thinks he ought to be doing, rather than "being himself" in obeying an imperious inner impulse, he has used a writing style which is marked by a "sincere" rather than a "knowing" use of cliché, the apparently unironic expression of sentiments verging on the banal, and a definite reluctance to employ anything beyond the simplest imagery. In the curious rendition of Red Hayes' and Jack Rhodes' 'A Satisfied Mind' with which *Saved* opens, we might easily imagine ourselves back with *Self Portrait*, that odd attempt to find his true self largely in the work of others.

That earlier statement of humility and simplicity led nowhere particularly worthwhile, but *Saved* is generally sterner and stronger stuff and contains many potentially fruitful starting-points for further development, should the apocalyptic day of whose imminence Dylan is clearly convinced (and who is to assert that he is wrong?) fail to supervene. Repeated listenings have forced me to change my mind about these songs in a way I have never experienced with any previous Dylan album. My initial reactions were almost wholly negative: the record seemed grey, joyless, monotonous and defeated, full of leaden fatigue, impelled forward by sheer force of will: calling to mind once again that line from 'Visions of Johanna': "Voices echo this is what salvation must be like after a while". First impressions should perhaps not be wholly discounted; they doubtless register an immediate response of the senses which

147

has some validity; but it is fair to say that I now feel that way only about a couple of tracks, notably 'Covenant Woman' and, to a lesser extent, 'What Can I Do for You?' Most of the other songs have a surging if sombre power which can often be very moving, while the record's more lugubrious aspects now seem to me to reflect with honesty the sense of being involved in an uphill struggle which is acknowledged in 'Saving Grace': "It gets discouraging at times, but I know I'll make it . . ." Dylan is still, in this, being true to his perennial vocation, the call to make the feeling real.

Saved also expresses a tension, which could yet prove very creative, between the huge release of spiritual energy occasioned by conversion, and a certain sense of being trapped. Whether or not the latter is consciously acknowledged by the will, it is certainly enacted artistically in, for instance, the frenzied repetitiveness of the chorus of 'Solid Rock': "I won't let go and I can't let go no more"; which at the end of the song, reiterated compulsively by the back-up singers, mimics an almost hysterical claustrophobia. The same feeling is powerfully communicated by the "Oh, I can't turn round" which Dylan seems spontaneously to interject into the relentless forward movement of 'Pressing On', one of the finest things on the album, the overall effect of which is to compel assent by the generous and full-blooded passion of its commitment. Equally good are 'In the Garden', a kind of brooding, tortured meditation to which some wonderfully sensitive keyboard work makes a notable contribution, and the confessional 'Saving Grace'. This song takes up the theme of salvation through faith from early death – "By this time I'd have thought that I would be sleeping / In a pine-box for all eternity" – and gives us Dylan's voice, which on this record is rawer and harsher in quality than ever before, at its most subtly expressive. Indeed, with this kind of music the quality of the voice assumes supreme importance, reducing the lyrics to little more than a vehicle for the articulation of pure feeling. Simon Frith has made the point excellently in a recent article: "Black religious music – gospel – articulates religious awe and fervour through an apparently spontaneous struggle *against* words. And in soul music, which developed out of gospel conventions, the term 'soul' refers to a quality of sincerity or intensity which can only be described in terms of how a singer sounds. The test of excellence in soul music is not the originality of the lyric, but the conviction with which it, the lyric, is sung. And the test of conviction is the singer's way with non-words."[1]

It must therefore be understood that Dylan's intentions are rather different here from those in the mainstream of his work, his voice now very much dominating his other talents: his sound speaks louder than his words. The complexity of feeling involved is not necessarily reduced by this development. The obverse side of the urge towards humility, for instance, is given spontaneous expression by the exultant edge which suddenly makes itself heard in his voice when he sings, in 'What Can I Do for You?', "And you've chosen me to be among the few" (a line which corresponds to that *one* upstretched hand towards which God points a finger on the cover). Humility *vis-à-vis* God is thus still offset by a certain arrogance *vis-à-vis* the rest of humanity; and for this reason the self-examination gestured towards in 'Are You Ready?', when he asks the question of himself, as well as of his hearers, does not entirely convince.

"As I look around this world all that I'm finding / Is the saving grace that's over me", Dylan sings in 'Saving Grace'; and compared with *Slow Train Coming* there is minimal evidence here of any urge to integrate personal faith in an overall view of the world. There are hints that he is experiencing difficulty in finding a role for himself within his new orientation, as when he tells Christ: "You've done it all and there's no more anyone can pretend to do" ('What Can I Do for You?'). Such a feeling must surely reflect a certain poverty in the particular evangelical tradition in which Dylan appears to have become involved. To suggest that the faith which has sustained Western civilization for most of two millenia offers the artist no valid field of action could only be wrong-headed. (It is interesting, incidentally, that the passage from Jeremiah (31.31) which is prominently displayed on the inside cover of *Saved* underlines the specifically Jewish nature of Dylan's concern for the figure of Christ, which was suggested as being significant in Chapter Four above. The text is one of the most important of those cited for proselytising purposes by early Jewish Christians to underline the continuity of the Christian revelation with the faith of their forefathers. In answer to accusations of betrayal made by their fellow Jews, they could use this prophecy to suggest that it was the main body of Jews who had betrayed themselves and their own past when they rejected the Messiah and thus put themselves at variance with the Divine plan.)[2]

Whatever its limitations, what *Saved* communicates with impressive power is the unanswerable authenticity of the inner experience which has taken command of Bob Dylan. This can clearly not be written off, for all the apparent crudity of some of its outward manifestations, as a temporary aberration which his fans can console themselves by predicting will in due course burn itself out, leaving them once more in untroubled possession of the Dylan of their desires. All the same, we may hope that this experience is fertile enough to give life to a richer and subtler religious vision than has found artistic expression in these latest Dylan songs. The seeds of such a vision do seem to be present in *Saved*, and it is satisfying to end with a few lines which hold a promise of depth yet to be explored:

> What kind of sign they need
> When it all come from within?
> When what's lost has been found,
> What's to come has already been?

I have generally used printed texts of Dylan's songs for purposes of quotation, as the words of recordings are occasionally not clear and because there may be a number of alternative recorded versions to choose from. However in a few instances where the printed text differs markedly from the most familiar recorded form I have preferred the latter. I have also sometimes commented on significant variations.

Texts used are *Writings and Drawings* and *The Songs of Bob Dylan from 1966 through 1975* (see Bibliography); and for later songs not included in these collections, the song books of individual albums.

Chapter One

1 Bob Dylan, *Tarantula*, New York 1971; Panther edition, St Albans 1973, pp. 86–87.
2 *Ibid.*, p. 98.
3 To Francis Taylor, 1965; quoted in *Bob Dylan: An Illustrated History*, produced by Michael Gross with a text by Robin Alexander, New York 1978, p. 54.
4 Michael Gray, *Song and Dance Man: The Art of Bob Dylan*, London and New York, 1972; Abacus edition, London 1973, p. 17.
5 George Steiner, *In Bluebeard's Castle*, London 1971, pp. 89–95.
6 H. M. McLuhan and Edmund Carpenter, *Explorations in Communication*, 1960; Introduction.
7 *Playboy*, March 1978, p. 73.
8 *Rolling Stone*, Nov. 16, 1978, p. 62.
9 Albert B. Lord, *The Singer of Tales*, Cambridge, Mass., 1960; quoted by David Buchan, *The Ballad and the Folk*, London 1972, p. 52.
10 Buchan, p. 58.
11 *Ibid.*, p. 64.
12 Ellen Willis, "Dylan", in *Cheetah*, 1967; reprinted in *Bob Dylan: A Retrospective*, ed. Craig McGregor, New York 1972; abridged Picador edition, London 1975, p. 150.
13 Jon Landau, 'John Wesley Harding', in *Crawdaddy!*, 1968; *Retrospective*, p. 164.
14 *Retrospective*, p. 136.

15 Paul Nelson, 'Newport Folk Festival, 1965', in *Sing Out!*, Nov. 1965; *Retrospective*, p. 56.
16 Ewan MacColl, 'A Youth of Mediocre Talent', in *Sing Out!*, Sept. 1965; *Retrospective*, p. 69.
17 Hamish Henderson, article on William McGonagall, in *Chapbook*, Vol. 2, No. 5, Aberdeen University Folksong Society, 1965 or 1966.
18 Michael Goldberg, 'Heaven can't Wait', *New Musical Express*, 17th. Nov. 1979.
19 Jann Wenner, *Rolling Stone*, Sept. 20, 1979, p. 94.
20 Interview with Nat Hentoff, *Playboy*, March 1966; *Retrospective*, p. 95.
21 Stuart Hoggard and Jim Shields, *Bob Dylan: An Illustrated Discography*, Oxford 1977; unnumberd page in 'Stop Press' section.
22 *Ibid.*, previous page.
23 Martin Esslin, *Brecht: A Choice of Evils*, London 1959, pp. 9, 96.
24 *Playboy*, Nov. 16, 1978, p. 88.
25 Gray, p. 21.
26 Craig McGregor in Introduction, *Retrospective*, p. 21; Gray, p. 233.
27 Interview with Nora Ephron and Susan Edmiston; *Retrospective*, p. 67.
28 'An Interview in Austin, Texas'; *Retrospective*, p. 113.

Chapter Two
1 Steven Goldberg, 'Bob Dylan and the Poetry of Salvation', 1970; *Retrospective*, p. 249.
2 *Rolling Stone*, Nov. 16, 1978, p. 60.
3 *Retrospective*, p. 164.
4 Anthony Scaduto, *Bob Dylan*, New York 1971; Abacus edition, London 1972, p. 249.
5 Introduction, *Retrospective*, p. 21.
6 *Tarantula*, pp. 28–30.
7 Gray, pp. 208–215.
8 *Rolling Stone*, Nov. 16, 1978, p. 60.
9 Gray, p. 288.
10 *Ibid.*, pp. 286–297.
11 *Ibid.*, p. 287.
12 *Rolling Stone*, Nov. 16, 1978, p. 60.

Chapter Three
1 See Scaduto, p. 145.
2 See for instance Gross, *Illustrated History*, p. 117; and Alan Rinzler, *Bob Dylan – The Illustrated Record*, New York 1978, p. 100.

NOTES ON SOURCES

3 *Illustrated History*, p. 118.
4 Gray, pp. 49–53.
5, 6, 7 *Rolling Stone*, Nov. 16, 1978, p. 60.

Chapter Four

1 Interview with Dylan by Ben Fong-Torres, 12 January 1974; printed in *Knockin' on Dylan's Door*, A Rolling Stone Book, New York 1974, p. 107.
2 Norman Cohn, *The Pursuit of the Millennium*, London 1957; Paladin Books, London 1970, p. 19.
3 Scaduto, p. 14.
4 See for instance *Playboy*, March 1978, p. 90.
5 Scaduto, p. 220.
6 *Playboy*, March 1978, p. 90.
7 I am substantially indebted to Andrew Greig for the ideas in this paragraph.
8 Gray, p. 177.
9 Matthew 19:30.
10 See Gray, p. 218.
11 *Ibid.*, pp. 184–188.
12 *Ibid.*, p. 186.
13 *Rolling Stone*, Nov. 16, 1978, p. 62.
14 Gray, p. 267.
15 Mark 15:26, and variants in the other Gospels.
16 Scaduto, p. 249.
17 *Retrospective*, p. 254.
18 Gray, pp. 50–53.
19 Scaduto, p. 251.
20 See Frank Kermode, *The Sense of an Ending*, New York, 1967; 1977 reprint, p. 25.
21 *Retrospective*, p. 255.
22 Scaduto, p. 257.
23 *Retrospective*, p. 172.
24 *Ibid.*, p. 178.
25 *Rolling Stone*, Nov. 16, 1978, p. 60.
26 Scaduto, p. 249.
27 *Rolling Stone*, Nov. 16, 1978, p. 60.
28 *Ibid.*, p. 60.
29 Kermode, p. 84.
30 Martin Dowle in *The Scotsman*, July 15, 1978.
31 *Playboy*, March 1978, p. 90.
32 *The Scotsman*, Sept. 8, 1979.
33 *Playboy*, March 1978, p. 90.
34 Scaduto, p. 220.
35 *Playboy*, March 1978, p. 74.

Chapter Five

1 *Retrospective*, pp. 116–118.
2 *Ibid.*, p. 63.
3 *Ibid.*, p. 150.
4 *Playboy*, March 1978, p. 73.
5 *Ibid.*, p. 73.
6 *Ibid.*, p. 69.
7 *Ibid.*, p. 70.
8 *Rolling Stone*, Nov. 16, 1978, p. 62.

Chapter Six

1 *Tarantula*, p. 87.
2 *Playboy*, March 1978, p. 64.
3 *Ibid.*, p. 69.
4 See Jon Landau, 'John Wesley Harding', *Retrospective*, p. 172.
5 *Rolling Stone*, Nov. 16, 1978, p. 60.
6 *Playboy*, March 1978, p. 74.
7 *Retrospective*, p. 164.
8 Dave Marsh, 'Rockers on the Road to Salvation', *Rolling Stone*, Oct. 18, 1978, p. 43.
9 *Retrospective*, p. 99.
10 Interview with Michael March, *Fusion*, Oct. 31, 1969; *Retrospective*, p. 191.
11 *Rolling Stone*, Nov. 16, 1978, p. 62.
12 *Playboy*, March 1978, pp. 74–78.
13 Alan Rinzler, *Bob Dylan: The Illustrated Record*, p. 119.
14 *Playboy*, March 1978, p. 80.
15 *Ibid.*, p. 82.
16 *Ibid.*, p. 80.
17 Michael Goldberg, *New Musical Express*, Nov. 17, 1979, p. 61.
18 *Playboy*, March 1978, p. 72.
19 Henry Miller, 'The Golden Age', in *Selected Prose II*, London 1965, pp. 432–433.
20 *Playboy*, March 1978, p. 80.
21 *Rolling Stone*, Nov. 16, 1978, p. 59.
22 *Ibid.*, p. 62.

Postscript

1 Simon Frith, 'Try to dig what we all say!', *The Listener*, June 26, 1980, pp. 822–3.
2 See Henry Chadwick, *The Early Church* (The Pelican History of the Church, Vol. 1), Harmondsworth, 1967, pp. 12–13.

DYLAN, BOB, *Tarantula*, Macmillan, New York, 1971; MacGibbon and Kee, London, 1971; Panther Books, St Albans, 1973.

DYLAN, BOB, *Writings and Drawings*, Knopf, New York, 1973; Jonathan Cape, London, 1973; Panther Books, St Albans, 1974.

DYLAN, BOB, *The Songs of Bob Dylan from 1966 through 1975*, Knopf, New York, 1976.

GRAY, MICHAEL, *Song and Dance Man: The Art of Bob Dylan*, Hart-Davis, MacGibbon, London, 1972; Dutton, New York, 1972; Abacus (Sphere Books), London, 1972.

GROSS, MICHAEL, *Bob Dylan: An Illustrated History*, with a text by Robert Alexander, Grosset and Dunlap, New York, 1978.

HOGGARD, STUART, and SHIELDS, JIM, *Bob Dylan: An Illustrated Discography*, Transmedia Express, Oxford, 1977.

McGREGOR, CRAIG (Ed.). *Bob Dylan: A Retrospective*, Morrow, New York, 1972; Picador (Pan Books), London, 1975.

MILES, *Bob Dylan*, Big O Publishing, London, 1978.

MILES (compiler), *Bob Dylan in his Own Words*, Omnibus Press, London 1978.

PENNEBAKER, D. A., *Don't Look Back*, Ballantine, New York, 1968.

PICKERING, STEPHEN, *Bob Dylan Approximately: A Portrait of the Jewish Poet in Search of God*, David McKay, New York, 1975.

RIBAKOVE, SY and BARBARA, *Folk-Rock: The Bob Dylan Story*, Dell, New York, 1966.

RINZLER, ALAN, *Bob Dylan: The Illustrated Record*, Harmony Books, New York, 1978.

ROLLING STONE (The Editors of), *Knockin' on Dylan's Door*, Pocket Books, New York, 1974.

SARLIN, BOB, *Turn It Up! (I Can't Hear the Words)*, Simon and Schuster, New York, 1973; Coronet Books, London, 1975.

SCADUTO, ANTHONY, *Bob Dylan*, Grosset and Dunlap, New York, 1971; W. H. Allen, London, 1972; Abacus (Sphere Books), London, 1972.

SHEPARD, SAM, *Rolling Thunder Logbook*, Viking Press, New York, 1977; Penguin Books, Harmondsworth, 1978.

VOICE WITHOUT RESTRAINT

THOMPSON, TOBY, *Positively Main Street*, Coward, McCann and Geoghegan, New York, 1971.

DISCOGRAPHY

This discography lists only the contents of officially recorded Dylan L.P.'s, for purposes of quick reference. Readers seeking details of singles, concert albums which feature Dylan with a number of other artists, or bootleg albums and tapes, are referred to the comprehensive *Bob Dylan: An Illustrated Discography*, by Stuart Hoggard and Jim Shields (see Bibliography).

BOB DYLAN (1962): *You're No Good* (Jesse Fuller); *Talkin' New York* (B. Dylan); *In My Time of Dyin'* (arr. B. Dylan); *Man of Constant Sorrow* (arr. B. Dylan); *Fixin' to Die* (Bukka White); *Pretty Peggy-O* (arr. B. Dylan); *Highway 51* (C. Jones); *Gospel Plow* (arr. B. Dylan); *Baby Let Me Follow You Down* (Rick Von Schmidt); *House of the Risin' Sun* (trad.); *Freight Train Blues* (trad.); *Song to Woody* (B. Dylan); *See That My Grave Is Kept Clean* (Blind Lemon Jefferson).

THE FREEWHEELIN' BOB DYLAN (1963): *Blowin' in the Wind; Girl From the North Country; Masters of War; Down the Highway; Bob Dylan's Blues; A Hard Rain's A-Gonna Fall; Don't Think Twice, It's All Right; Bob Dylan's Dream; Oxford Town; Talking World War III Blues; Corinna, Corrina* (arr. B. Dylan); *Honey, Just Allow Me One More Chance* (H. Thomas and B. Dylan); *I Shall Be Free*. All by B. Dylan except as otherwise indicated.

THE TIMES THEY ARE A-CHANGIN' (1964): *The Times They Are A-Changin'; Ballad of Hollis Brown; With God on Our Side; One Too Many Mornings; North Country Blues; Only a Pawn in Their Game; Boots of Spanish Leather; When the Ship Comes In; The Lonesome Death of Hattie Carroll; Restless Farewell*. All by B. Dylan.

ANOTHER SIDE OF BOB DYLAN (1964): *All I Really Want to Do; Black Crow Blues; Spanish Harlem Incident; Chimes of Freedom; I Shall Be Free No. 10; To Ramona; Motorpsycho Nitemare; My Back Pages; I Don't Believe You; Ballad in Plain D; It Ain't Me, Babe*. All by B. Dylan.

BRINGING IT ALL BACK HOME (1965); *Subterranean Homesick Blues; She Belongs To Me; Maggie's Farm; Love Minus Zero/No Limit; Outlaw Blues; On the Road Again; Bob Dylan's 115th Dream; Mr Tambourine Man; Gates of Eden; It's Alright, Ma (I'm Only Bleeding); It's All Over Now, Baby Blue*. All by B. Dylan.

SELECTED BIBLIOGRAPHY AND DISCOGRAPHY

HIGHWAY 61 REVISITED (1965): *Like A Rolling Stone; Tombstone Blues; It Takes a Lot to Laugh, It Takes a Train to Cry; From a Buick 6; Ballad of a Thin Man; Queen Jane Approximately; Highway 61 Revisited; Just Like Tom Thumb's Blues; Desolation Row.* All by B. Dylan.

BLONDE ON BLONDE (1966): *Rainy Day Women Nos. 12 & 35; Pledging My Time; Visions of Johanna; One of Us Must Know (Sooner or Later); I Want You; Stuck Inside of Mobile with the Memphis Blues Again; Leopard-Skin Pill-Box Hat; Just Like a Woman; Most Likely You Go Your Way and I'll Go Mine; Temporary Like Achilles; Absolutely Sweet Marie; Fourth Time Around; Obviously Five Believers; Sad Eyed Lady of the Lowlands.* All by B. Dylan.

BOB DYLAN'S GREATEST HITS (1967): *Blowin' in the Wind; It Ain't Me, Babe; The Times They Are A-Changin'; Mr Tambourine Man; She Belongs to Me; It's All Over Now, Baby Blue; Subterranean Homesick Blues; One of Us Must Know (Sooner or Later); Like A Rolling Stone; Just Like a Woman; Rainy Day Women Nos. 12 & 35; I Want You.* All by B. Dylan.

JOHN WESLEY HARDING (1968): *John Wesley Harding; As I Went Out One Morning; I Dreamed I Saw St Augustine; All Along the Watchtower; The Ballad of Frankie Lee and Judas Priest; Drifter's Escape; Dear Landlord; I Am a Lonesome Hobo; I Pity the Poor Immigrant; The Wicked Messenger; Down Along the Cove; I'll Be Your Baby Tonight.* All by B. Dylan.

NASHVILLE SKYLINE (1969): *Girl From the North Country* (with J. Cash); *Nashville Skyline Rag; To Be Alone with You; I Threw It All Away; Peggy Day; Lay Lady Lay; One More Night; Tell Me that It Isn't True; Country Pie; Tonight I'll Be Staying Here with You.* All by B. Dylan.

SELF PORTRAIT (1970): *All the Tired Horses* (B. Dylan); *Alberta No. 1* (B. Dylan); *I Forgot More than You'll Ever Know* (C. A. Null); *Days of 49* (Frank Warner); *Early Mornin' Rain* (Gordon Lightfoot); *In Search of Little Sadie* (B. Dylan); *Let it Be Me* (M. Curtis, G. Becaud, P. Delano); *Little Sadie* (B. Dylan); *Woogie Boogie* (B. Dylan); *Belle Isle* (B. Dylan); *Living the Blues* (B. Dylan); *Like A Rolling Stone* (B. Dylan); *Copper Kettle* (trad.); *Gotta Travel On* (P: Clayton); *Blue Moon* (Richard Rodgers, Lorenz Hart); *The Boxer* (Paul Simon); *The Mighty Quinn (Quinn the Eskimo)* (B. Dylan); *Take Me As I Am (Or Let Me Go)* (B. Bryant); *Take a Message to Mary* (B. and F. Bryant); *It Hurts Me Too* (B. Dylan); *Minstrel Boy* (B. Dylan); *She Belongs to Me* (B. Dylan); *Wigwam* (B. Dylan); *Alberta No. 2* (B. Dylan).

NEW MORNING (1970): *If Not For You; Day of the Locusts; Time Passes Slowly; Went to See the Gypsy; Winterlude; If Dogs Run Free; New Morning; Sign on the Window; One More Weekend; The Man in Me; Three Angels; Father of Night.* All by B. Dylan.

MORE BOB DYLAN GREATEST HITS (1971): *Watching the River Flow; Don't Think Twice, It's All Right; Lay Lady Lay; Stuck Inside of Mobile; I'll Be Your Baby Tonight; All I Really Want to Do; My Back Pages; Maggie's Farm; Tonight I'll Be Staying Here with You; Positively 4th Street; All Along the Watchtower; The Mighty Quinn (Quinn the Eskimo); Just Like Tom Thumb's Blues; A Hard Rain's A-Gonna Fall; If Not for You; New Morning; Tomorrow is a Long Time; When I Paint my Masterpiece; I Shall Be Released; You Ain't Goin' Nowhere; Down in the Flood.* All by B. Dylan.

PAT GARRETT & BILLY THE KID (Soundtrack) (1973): *Main Title Theme (Billy); Cantina Theme (Workin' for the Law); Billy 1; Bunkhouse Theme; River Theme; Turkey Chase; Knockin' on Heaven's Door; Final Theme; Billy 4; Billy 7.* All by B. Dylan.

DYLAN (1973): *Lily of the West* (E. Davies, J. Peterson); *Can't Help Falling in Love* (G. Weiss, H. Peretti, L. Creatore); *Sarah Jane* (trad.); *The Ballad of Ira Hayes* (P. La Farge); *Mr Bojangles* (J. J. Walker); *Mary Ann* (trad.); *Big Yellow Taxi* (J. Mitchell); *A Fool Such as I* (B. Trader); *Spanish is the Loving Tongue* (trad.).

PLANET WAVES (1974): *On a Night Like This; Going, Going, Gone; Tough Mama; Hazel; Something There is About You; Forever Young, Forever Young; Dirge; You Angel You; Never Say Goodbye; Wedding Song.* All by B. Dylan.

BEFORE THE FLOOD (with The Band) (1974): *Most Likely You Go Your Way (and I'll Go Mine); Lay Lady Lay; Rainy Day Women Nos. 12 & 35; Knockin' on Heaven's Door; It Ain't Me, Babe; Ballad of a Thin Man; Up on Cripple Creek* (R. Robertson); *I Shall Be Released; Endless Highway* (R. Robertson); *The Night They Drove Old Dixie Down* (R. Robertson); *Stage Fright* (R. Robertson); *Don't Think Twice, It's All Right; Just Like a Woman; It's Alright, Ma (I'm Only Bleeding); The Shape I'm In* (R. Robertson); *When You Awake* (R. Robertson, Manuel); *The Weight* (R. Robertson); *All Along the Watchtower; Highway 61 Revisited; Like A Rolling Stone; Blowin' in the Wind.* All by B. Dylan except as otherwise indicated.

BLOOD ON THE TRACKS (1975): *Tangled Up in Blue; Simple Twist of*

Fate; You're a Big Girl Now; Idiot Wind; You're Gonna Make Me Lonesome When You Go; Meet Me in the Morning; Lily, Rosemary and the Jack of Hearts; If You See Her, Say Hello; Shelter from the Storm; Buckets of Rain. All by B. Dylan.

THE BASEMENT TAPES (with The Band) (1975): *Odds and Ends; Orange Juice Blues (Blues for Breakfast)* (R. Manuel); *Million Dollar Bash; Yazoo Street Scandal* (J. R. Robertson); *Going to Acapulco; Katie's Been Gone* (J. R. Robertson, R. Manuel); *Lo and Behold; Bessie Smith* (R. Danko, J. R. Robertson); *Clothes Line Saga; Apple Suckling Tree; Please, Mrs Henry; Tears of Rage* (B. Dylan, R. Manuel); *Too Much of Nothing; Yea! Heavy and a Bottle of Bread; Ain't No More Cane* (trad., arr. The Band); *Crash on the Levee (Down in the Flood); Ruben Remus* (J. R. Robertson, R. Manuel); *Tiny Montgomery; You Ain't Goin' Nowhere; Don't Ya Tell Henry; Nothing Was Delivered; Open the Door, Homer; Long Distance Operator; This Wheel's on Fire* (B. Dylan, R. Danko). By B. Dylan except as otherwise indicated.

DESIRE (1975): *Hurricane; Isis; Mozambique; One More Cup of Coffee (Valley Below)* (B. Dylan); *Oh, Sister; Joey; Romance in Durango; Black Diamond Bay; Sara* (B. Dylan). All by B. Dylan and J. Levy except as otherwise indicated.

HARD RAIN (1976): *Maggie's Farm; One Too Many Mornings; Stuck Inside of Mobile; Oh, Sister* (B. Dylan, J. Levy); *Lay Lady Lay; Shelter from the Storm; You're a Big Girl Now; I Threw It All Away; Idiot Wind.* All by B. Dylan except as otherwise indicated.

STREET-LEGAL (1978): *Changing of the Guards; New Pony; No Time to Think; Baby Stop Crying; Is Your Love in Vain?; Señor (Tales of Yankee Power): True Love Tends to Forget; We Better Talk This Over; Where Are You Tonight? (Journey Through Dark Heat).* All by B. Dylan.

BOB DYLAN AT BUDOKAN (1978): *Mr Tambourine Man; Shelter from the Storm; Love Minus Zero / No Limit; Ballad of a Thin Man; Don't Think Twice, It's All Right; Maggie's Farm; One More Cup of Coffee (Valley Below); Like A Rolling Stone; I Shall Be Released; Is Your Love in Vain?; Going, Going, Gone; Blowin' in the Wind; Just Like a Woman; Oh, Sister* (B. Dylan and J. Levy); *Simple Twist of Fate; All Along the Watchtower; I Want You; All I Really Want to Do; Knockin' on Heaven's Door; It's Alright, Ma (I'm Only Bleeding); Forever Young; The Times they Are A-Changin'.* All by B. Dylan except as otherwise indicated.

VOICE WITHOUT RESTRAINT

SLOW TRAIN COMING (1979): *Gotta Serve Somebody; Precious Angel; I Believe in You; Slow Train; Gonna Change my Way of Thinking; Do Right to Me Baby (Do Unto Others); When You Gonna Wake Up; Man Gave Names to All the Animals; When He Returns.* All by B. Dylan.

SAVED (1980): *A Satisfied Mind* (Red Hayes and Jack Rhodes); *Saved* (B. Dylan and Tim Drummond); *Covenant Woman; What Can I Do for You?; Solid Rock; Pressing On; In the Garden; Saving Grace; Are You Ready?* All by B. Dylan except as otherwise indicated.

Index

INDEX

INDEX

INDEX